ISBN 978-1-333-37094-7
PIBN 10496317

This book is a reproduction of an important historical work. Forgotten Books uses state-of-the-art technology to digitally reconstruct the work, preserving the original format whilst repairing imperfections present in the aged copy. In rare cases, an imperfection in the original, such as a blemish or missing page, may be replicated in our edition. We do, however, repair the vast majority of imperfections successfully; any imperfections that remain are intentionally left to preserve the state of such historical works.

English
Français
Deutsche
Italiano
Español
Português

www.forgottenbooks.com

Mythology Photography **Fiction**
Fishing Christianity **Art** Cooking
Essays Buddhism Freemasonry
Medicine **Biology** Music **Ancient
Egypt** Evolution Carpentry Physics
Dance Geology **Mathematics** Fitness
Shakespeare **Folklore** Yoga Marketing
Confidence Immortality Biographies
Poetry **Psychology** Witchcraft
Electronics Chemistry History **Law**
Accounting **Philosophy** Anthropology
Alchemy Drama Quantum Mechanics
Atheism Sexual Health **Ancient History**
Entrepreneurship Languages Sport
Paleontology Needlework Islam
Metaphysics Investment Archaeology
Parenting Statistics Criminology
Motivational

PERCY'S

POCKET DICTIONARY OF

CONEY ISLAND

AN INDEX AND GUIDE TO

RAILROAD AND STEAMBOAT ROUTES, HOTELS, AMUSEMENTS,
RESTAURANTS, HISTORICAL AND GEOGRAPHICAL FACTS,
AND ALL OTHER THINGS IN AND ABOUT THIS
RESORT; WITH AN APPENDIX ON BATH-
ING, SWIMMING, AND THE
SUMMER STARS

EDITED AND COMPILED BY

TOWNSEND PERCY

With Maps and Illustrations

SEASON OF 1880

NEW YORK
F. LEYPOLDT, 13 AND 15 PARK ROW
1880

THE JOHN A. GRAY PRESS,
16 and 18 Jacob Street,
NEW YORK.

PREFATORY NOTE.

Careful consideration has been given to the choice of subjects treated in this little book, and it has been my aim to make it as complete and trustworthy as "Appletons' Dictionary of New York," which I compiled, and which was the first hand-book of the kind printed in America. To this end nothing that appears in the body of the Dictionary is in any sense an advertisement, and no payment has been or will be received for it, either directly or indirectly. Whatever is an advertisement distinctly appears as such.

It is too much to hope that entire accuracy could be secured in a first edition. Any corrections of errors which may be observed, and any suggestions which may tend to the improvement of the Dictionary will be thankfully received with the view of profiting by them in subsequent editions.

I avail myself of this opportunity to thank those who have kindly assisted me by their prompt response to applications for information. TOWNSEND PERCY.

HOW TO USE THE DICTIONARY.

For *special* information turn to the name of person or place, or to the very word expressing the object on which you want to be informed. If not given under that word, reference is made to the word where it is.

For *general* information and *starting-points*, turn to the articles, "Amusements," "Geography," "History," "How to See Coney Island in One Day," "Picnics," "Trip to Coney Island," "Hotels," "Restaurants," "Dinners," etc., which give the cues for further information.

THE APPENDIX

Contains Hints on Bathing and Swimming; Surf styles; Directions how to find the Summer Stars; a Summer Calendar, for sun, moon and high water; and Time-Tables for Railroads and Steamboats.

SECTIONAL MAP

OF

CONEY ISLAND.

IN QUARTER-MILE SQUARES.

———

I.—(Left-Hand Page.) *West End.*

II.—(Right-Hand Page.) *East End.*

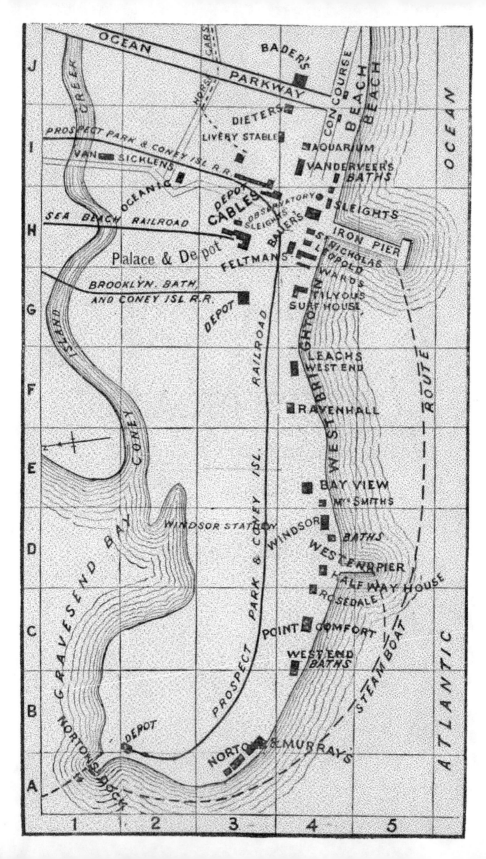

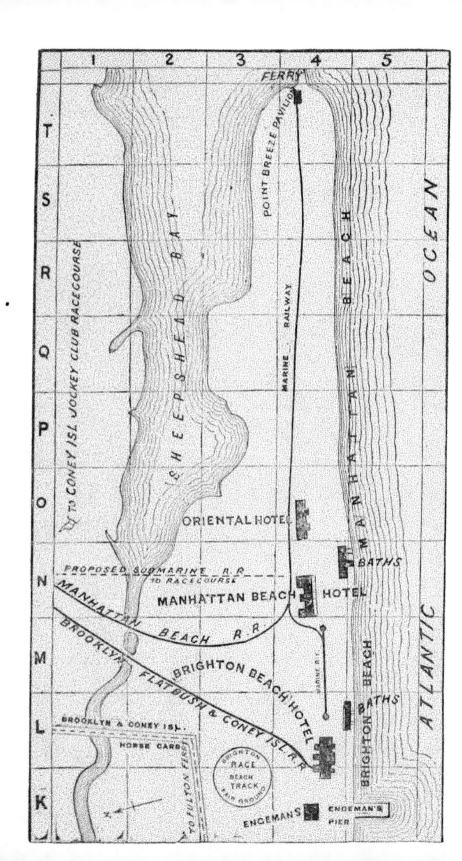

PERCY'S

POCKET DICTIONARY OF

CONEY ISLAND.

Amphitheatre.—[Map, N4]—A portion of the Manhattan Beach Bathing Pavilion on the west is inclosed on three sides but open toward the ocean, and is fitted with tiers of seats rising one above another nearly to the roof. A band of music plays here during the afternoon and evening, and it affords a sheltered and luxurious resting-place from which to watch the amusing antics or petty mishaps of the bathers, and to make studies of human nature as nearly "in a state of nature" as may be. The admission is ten cents, but it is free to those who purchase bath tickets.

Amusements.—In a general way the amusements at Coney Island would appear to be those peculiar to and naturally afforded by seaside resorts ; but the daily congregation of thousands of people of varying tastes has led to the establishment by speculators of any number of diversions not ordinarily attainable at the seashore. The average man, bent only upon obtaining relaxation and rational amusement, will find it naturally enough in the alternate contemplation of the ocean, and the people by whom he is surrounded, or in listening to the orchestral music, and will perhaps supplement these quiet pleasures with a dip in the surf and a well-chosen repast.   Mothers and children will find an inexhaustible fund of amusement in patrolling or camping down upon the sand at the water's edge, where the little ones can make futile efforts to reach China by virtue of a toy shovel and *via* perpendicular excavations in the white-sanded shore.

At a place like Coney Island, however, easily and cheaply accessible from several great cities, the throng of visitors is sure to include a proportion of restless spirits who are not satisfied with enjoyments or pleasures of so prosaic a nature, and among these are many who visit the Island, over-exert themselves, expose themselves recklessly to the sun, bathe too frequently, or remain too long in the water, fill their stomachs with unwholesome food, indulge too freely in alcoholic beverages, and who find on returning home that they have aching heads and limbs or disordered stomachs, from which results they draw the very natural inference that the salt air does not agree with their constitutions.

The list of amusements naturally begins with bathing.   Music is to be heard at or near almost every building along the beach ; billiard-tables and bowling-alleys are to be found at several of the principal hotels ; shooting-galleries are everywhere , archery practice and Aunt Sally at various places along the beach ; croquet-grounds at Brighton and West Brighton, and dancing at Feltman's Pavilion at West Brighton.   Fishing, sailing, and rowing may be had at Point Breeze, at the extreme east of the island.   Exhibitions of fireworks are given at some one of the hotels almost every night.   There are several "shows," the principal ones, the Aquarium, Feltman's Theatre, the Midgets' Palace, the Camera Obscura, and the Observatory. There are two race-courses at the beach, belonging to the Coney Island Jockey Club and to Engeman, where good racing takes place at stated intervals. If you can find any pleasure in having your picture taken, that is obtainable ; and the greatest pleasure may be derived at table if you know what to eat, and the greatest discomfort if you do not.

☞ *Each of the amusements mentioned above will be found described at length under its appropriate heading.*

Aquarium (The)—[Map, I4]—is contained in a two-story frame building, directly east of Vandeveer's Hotel and the Plaza at West Brighton. It contains a good collection of fish and marine curiosities in tanks, and Tom Thumb and his troupe, which comprises an assortment of trained birds, a man-fish, a woman-fish, " Punch and Judy," that child's wonder, and other similar attractions. There are two large halls in the building, which is about 158 feet long and 100 feet deep. In the cupola, which surmounts the structure, is placed a steam orchestrion of " 100-instrument power." The place is open daily from 11 A.M. to 10 P.M., and the admission is ten cents to all parts of the building. At the east end is a space set apart for a Rhode Island clambake (*see* CLAMBAKES). The Police Headquarters are also in this building.

Arbuckle, Cornet Soloist, plays at (Cable's) Ocean View Hotel (which *see*).

Bader's Hotel.—*See* GRAND CENTRAL HOTEL.

Barber-Shops will be found at Manhattan, Brighton, Cable's and other large hotels.

Bath is a suburban village on the Long Island shore of the Narrows, about two miles below Fort Hamilton. It is one of the old Dutch settlements on Long Island, and contains a number of substantial and roomy houses of the old style. Good board can be obtained here at reasonable rates, and Coney Island reached in a few moments. Bath can be reached by trains of the Brooklyn, Bath & Coney Island Railway from Greenwood—connection to be made by taking Greenwood horse-cars from Fulton, Wall, and South ferries, and by boat from the Battery.

Bathing.—A very large proportion of the visitors to Coney Island find the source of their greatest pleasure in the surf-bathing, and if care is exercised the profit equals the pleasure. There can be no question but that the bathing-houses and arrangements at the Manhattan Bathing Pavilion are the most luxurious on the island, but others approach them very nearly, and many persons find in the retirement and privacy of less frequented portions of the beach ample compensation for the somewhat primitive character of the facilities offered. Except that at the west end but little care is given to clearing the beach of the drift-wood and seaweed cast up by the tide, there is little to choose in the matter of location, as from one extremity of the island to the other, the beach is equally smooth and safe, and the magnificent surf of the same character. The old-fashioned bathing-houses are strung along the beach from West Brighton to the west end, under the direction of innumerable small hotel-keepers and speculators, and between these there is very little to choose. The uniform price for the use of a bathing-house and dress is 25 cents, but at a few of the rude places toward the west end, 15 or 20 cents only is charged, but 25 cents is the maximum price at the best places. At the Manhattan Beach Bathing Pavilion, Brighton Beach Bathing Pavilion, and at the Iron Pier, will be found the most luxurious bathing facilities, and fair bathing accommodations are to be had at Feltman's and at Tilyou's Surf House, the latter affected by mothers and children. Details in regard to all these places will be found under their respective headings. (*See also*, HINTS ON BATHING. *in Appendix*.)

Bathing-suits.—According to Dr. Packard, the material should always be woollen, and flannel is decidedly the best. Those who do not swim will find it more comfortable to protect the skin of the arms and legs from sunburn by having the sleeves come down to the wrists and the trousers to the ankle. Swimmers will find it much more convenient, as well as safer, to wear short sleeves, wide at the shoulder, and trousers or drawers reaching only to the knees. There is nothing more hampering to one who is becoming a little tired than a heavy dress ; and it might make the difference between danger and safety in the case of a man who had overestimated his powers, or who had been carried out farther than he intended.

For women.—According to Dr. Durant, the bathing-dress should be made of a woollen fabric, the warp of which is worsted, the woof serge. We particularly insist upon woollen as the material to be worn, as it retains the heat of the body, and therefore prevents a too rapid evaporation. Maroon and blue are the proper colors, as they resist the corrosive and bleaching effects of the salt-water. The dress should consist essentially of two parts—a pair of pantaloons and a blouse.

The latter should not fit too tightly ; the sleeves fastened loosely at the wrist, and slits cut in the garment just below the arm-pits. A belt of the same woollen stuff is attached to the blouse to retain it at the waist. The pantaloons should be short, upheld by suspenders, and should not be buttoned too tightly to the legs, as circulation would be thereby impeded. (*See also, in the Appendix,* SURF STYLES *for* 1880.)

Bathing-hats.—A broad-brimmed straw hat may be worn, but, says Dr. Durant, all coverings (such as oil-skin caps, so commonly worn by ladies to prevent the hair being wet), preventing a free perspiration on the scalp, are injurious, since the secretions from the skin are stopped, and the head has to perform more than its share of the work ; and also, on account of the increased cerebral circulation, all possible care should be taken to keep that part of the body at its habitual temperature.

Bathing Shoes afford for women and children an excellent safeguard against the bruising of the feet by shells or pebbles, as well as against the heat of the sand, which is often intense. (*See also, in Appendix,* SURF STYLES *for* 1880.)

Bauer's Hotel.—See WEST BRIGHTON BEACH HOTEL.

Billiards.—Devotees of this game will find tables at hotels of almost every grade on the island. A word of warning : do not bet with gentlemanly strangers, as their game is apt to improve marvellously at critical moments. There are no billiard-tables at Manhattan Beach, but at the Brighton Hotel Maurice Daly has sixteen good tables, and there are also tables at Cable's, Vanderveer's, the Sea Beach, Feltman's and many other hotels.

The prices are about the same as those charged at first-class rooms in New York.

Boarding-Houses.—There are really no board-ing-houses proper along the beach, although boarders are taken at some of the small and unattractive places at the West End. There is, of course, a variation in the rates at the principal hotels for persons who remain any considerable part of the season, and board at some of the hotels near West Brighton may be had at from $15 to $20 per week. At almost all the hotels, however, you hire your rooms and take your meals *à la carte*, an expensive mode of living. There is really no such thing, at present, as good board at reasonable rates to be had at Coney Island. At Bath (which *see*) good board may be had at fair rates, and it is within a few minutes' ride of the island.

Boating.—*See* SAILING and ROWING.

Bowling.—At the Brighton Beach Hotel, at the Sea Beach Palace, and at Feltman's Hotel, will be found excellent bowling-alleys, where those who care for this amusement may disport themselves at about the ordinary prices charged in New York.

Brighton Beach is the name given to that portion of the Island between the Concourse and Manhattan Beach. It is the very heart of the Island and is the resort par excellence of Brooklyn people. It is easily reached from that city by the superb Ocean Parkway and the Concourse in carriages. The buildings here are the Brighton Hotel, the Brighton Bathing Pavilion, and Engeman's Hotel and Pier, which are virtually a part of the Brighton Beach. Shooting galleries, peddlers, fortune-tellers, shows, etc., are allowed on the beach, and if they are objectionable to some people yet they serve to give animation and color to the scenes.

Brighton Beach Bathing Pavilion — [Map, L4]—is east of the Brighton Beach Hotel, and is a large two-story building. An addition 50 x 80 feet has been made during the past year, and the general character of the bathing facilities greatly improved. There are now about 1200 bath-rooms, all on the second floor, the ladies' rooms on the east and the gentlemen's on the west. From each side an arched bridge is thrown out over the sand to the water's edge, thus enabling bathers to reach the water without crossing the beach. A life-raft or catamaran in charge of an able seaman is kept constantly in the water, and life-lines are in abundance. The bathing-grounds are illumined at night by an electric light. The price charged for use of bathing-suit and room is 25 cents, and for the care of valuables there is an extra charge of 10 cents, the system being the same as that in vogue at the Manhattan Beach Bathing Pavilion (which *see*). There are also hot and cold salt-water · baths in private rooms at 50 cents each. On the lower floor of this pavilion are a restaurant and bar and the Midgets' Palace (which *see*).

Brighton Beach Fair Grounds.—*See* ENGEMAN'S RACE-COURSE.

Brighton Beach Railroad.—*See* BROOKLYN, FLATBUSH AND CONEY ISLAND RAILROAD.

Brighton Hotel [Map L4] is the chief hotel at Brighton Beach, and is the terminus of the Brooklyn, Flatbush and Coney Island Railroad, commonly called the "Brighton Beach Road." It is a large and airy framed structure, 525 feet long, and varies from three to five stories in height. A wide porch on the first and a piazza on the second floor extend around the building, furnishing a fine promenade for the guests. On the first floor are commodious dining-rooms, where 2000 persons can be served at one time, and 20,000 persons fed in one day. There is a bar-room in the rear, and a billiard-room containing sixteen tables, under the direction of Maurice Daly, and four bowling-alleys in the basement. The upper floors are reserved exclusively for the guests of the hotel proper. Here are about 400 sleeping-rooms, furnished with Eastlake furniture, handsomely carpeted, and finished in natural wood. There is gas and running water in every room. The sewerage of the hotel is by means of a series of iron tanks, in which the waste is deodorized and separated, the water discharged into the creek, and the solid matter made into fertilizers. The hotel is leased by James Breslin, of the Gilsey House, New York, and is managed by H. A. Chadwick, formerly of the Girard in Philadelphia, Baldwin in San Francisco, and Willard's Hotel, Washington. The house is conducted on both the American and European plans, so-called. Rooms are rented without board at from $2 to $5 per day, and the standard rate with board is $5 per day. Slight concessions from these rates are made to parties desiring to remain for several weeks. An excellent *table-d'hôte* dinner is served daily, including wine, at $1.50 a head. The Bullion Club and the New York Club have branch club-rooms at this house. The grounds in front of the hotel are beautifully laid out in greensward, intersected by numerous walks, and from a large music-stand directly in front of the house concerts are given every afternoon and evening by Ad. Neuendorf's orchestra. The hotel is a place peculiarly affected by Brooklyn people, and is a capital family resort. The cooking and service is of the best, and the most perfect order and attention are guaranteed.

Brooklyn and Coney Island Horse Railroad starts from Fulton Ferry, and the line is commonly known as the "Jay, Smith and Ninth Street Cars," indicating the streets through which the road runs. The road skirts Prospect Park, and reaches the beach by running parallel with the Ocean Parkway on the west. The terminus at the island is at the Grand Union Hotel, in the rear of West Brighton Beach. The time occupied in the journey is more than an hour and a half. The fare is twenty-five cents excursion from the Fulton Ferry, and fifteen cents excursion from the City Line at Prospect Park.

Brooklyn, Bath and Coney Island Railroad starts from the main entrance to Greenwood Cemetery, and runs to a depot in the rear of West Brighton Beach, stopping *en route* at Locust Grove on Gravesend Bay to receive passengers from New York by steamer. The depot at Greenwood is accessible by horse-cars from the Brooklyn side of Fulton, Wall, South and Hamilton Ferries. This is sometimes called Gunther's road.—☞ *See* TIME-TABLE *in Appendix.*

Brooklyn, Flatbush and Coney Island Railroad starts from the Long Island Railroad depot at Flatbush and Atlantic Avenues, and stops at Franklin Avenue, Bergen Street and Prospect Park, Brooklyn. The road is very straight, running almost due south from the city line, and is of the average gauge. The rolling stock is excellent, and the engines of the same large size as those run on the Pennsylvania Railroad. This is commonly called the Brighton Beach Road. The Flatbush Avenue station is accessible from Fulton Ferry *via* Flatbush Avenue horse-cars in about twenty minutes. From New York this road is also accessible *via* the Long Island Railroad from Hunter's Point, reached by ferries from Wall Street, James Slip, and East 34th Street. Palace cars are run on this route.— ☞ *See* TIME-TABLE *in Appendix.*

Cable's Hotel.—*See* OCEAN VIEW HOTEL.

Camera Obscura (The) is contained in a small octagonal building near the centre of the plaza at West Brighton Beach. An admission fee of ten cents is charged, and about a dozen persons can stand in the room at one time. When the doors are closed a series of moving pictures of the beach which are simply charming, are thrown on a revolving disk. The colors are heightened in brilliancy, the outlines delicately sharpened, and the miniatures are so distinct that the movements of the eyes and lips of persons half a mile away can be observed distinctly. This is one of the most pleasing as well as instructive sights on the island, and has a practical value since any person losing children or friends can locate them at once if they are anywhere on the beach.

Carlberg's Orchestra plays at the Sea Beach Hotel (which *see*).

Carnarsie, a village on Jamaica Bay, Long Island, noted for its fish and clams, with which the bay abounds, and from which the inhabitants derive their means of living. There are one or two fair hotels, and in summer steamers ply between it and Rockaway on the opposite side of the bay. It can be reached from East New York by way of the Brooklyn and Rockaway Beach Railway—connections to be made by Brooklyn horse-cars from Fulton, Roosevelt, and Grand Street ferries, and by rapid transit trains from South Ferry. The time occupied in getting there is something over an hour. Fare for the round trip, twenty cents.

Cautions.—*See* articles on BATHING and SWIMMING (Cautionary), *in Appendix.*

Children.—*See* AMUSEMENTS ; and *in Appendix,* under HINTS ON BATHING.

Children's Toy Shovels and Pails can be bought at the stands in the main halls of Manhattan, Brighton, and other hotels, and at outside stands scattered along the beach. Prices range from ten to twenty cents.

Chowder.—*See* RESTAURANTS.

Clambakes, popularly so-called, are a myth, since the Coney Island Clambake consists of roasted clams, and the Rhode Island Clambake of a variety of steam-cooked food. Without stopping to quarrel with these misnomers, however, it may be safely asserted that while they are both luxuries in their way, the Coney Island Clambake is no more to be compared with the Rhode Island Clambake, than corned pork with canvas-back duck. The first is achieved by roasting hard-shell clams in hot wood ashes until the shells crack with the heat, when they are served piping hot, and entrusted, with a confidence which is usually misplaced, to the hungry guest. If he goes not the way to eat clams he will perhaps deluge them with vinegar or pepper or salt or catsup, or heaven knows what atrocious conglomeration of condiments and sauces, and effectually extinguish the identity of the precious clam. If, on the other hand, he is a true lover of this choice mollusk, he will melt a table-spoonful of butter, add a pinch of salt and the juice of half a lemon, preserving carefully any of the juice of the clam which is obtainable, and after having extracted the roast clams from the heap of shells and ashes in front of him, dip them in this sauce, and eat them with dry French bread and thankfulness of heart. Roast clams, as these are properly called, are by no means to be despised. A Rhode Island clambake in its perfection, however, offers to the epicure such a feast as Brillat Savarin's genius in its wildest flights never even dreamed of. The mode of cooking the edibles which go to make up this toothsome repast will in great measure explain the unique merits which the cooked food possesses. A huge wood fire having been built on a flat stone oven, the stones in time become nearly white hot and the wood reduced to living coals. This oven is then smothered with a heap of fresh seaweed, drawn from the water, damp, salt, dripping sweet brine and gemmed with tiny shells. Upon this couch thus prepared a layer of soft shell clams, oysters, spring chickens (split as if for broiling), green corn, and sweet potatoes are reverently laid to rest, another layer of seaweed placed upon them, a second layer of similar food on that, and so on to the end. Presently the whole mass, penetrated by the great heat of the oven, begins to steam gently, delicious odors mingle with the sea breeze, and, if you can appreciate the esoteric poetry of the clam, you give yourself up to dreams of bliss unutterable, with the profoundly consoling underlying assurance that when yon mass of seaweed gives up its prey, all your dreams will be more than realized. When the " bake " is ready to open, the food will be found steamed to a turn, the oysters and clams opening their shell-mouths to be removed, the dainty flesh of the chickens ready to drop at a touch from their bones, the " Carliny " potatoes bursting their jackets, the milky kernels of the corn swollen with a plethora of milky sweetness, and the whole delicately seasoned with the briny exhalations of. the perished seaweed. You will know how to make the attack without instruction, and the only permissible accompaniment to such a feast is the very dryest of " Extra Dry." It is manifestly im- possible to attain this degree of perfection where the " bake " is concocted by rude hands for hire, but at Point Breeze Pavilion, accessible *via* Ma- rine Railway, fare five cents, a capital Rhode Island Clambake is served at five P.M. daily, at seventy- five cents a head. Drink good Milwaukee lager with it. At the Aquarium also a Rhode Island clambake of fair quality is served daily (all day) at fifty cents a head. Roast Clams are to be had at every restaurant on the island at a uniform price of forty cents a dish. Those served at Rav- enhall (which see) are highly esteemed by male connoisseurs.

Clams.—*See* CLAMBAKES ; DINNERS ; FISH DIN- NERS ; RESTAURANTS.

Clothing for the Sea-Shore.—In view of the frequent and sometimes sudden changes in weather which occur at the seaside during the summer months it may be of value to those con- templating a stay of several days at the beach to heed the following suggestion of Dr. Packard, as regards the clothing most suitable for the place and season : " It is better always to wear woollen clothing, however light and loose in texture; and thin gauze merino undershirts, worn next the skin, afford a great safeguard against the checking of perspiration, or chilling in case of a sudden fall of the temperature. Caution should also be observed at night, when it is often imprudent to walk or drive without extra wraps at hand." *See also* BATHING-SUITS.

Clubs.—The Coney Island Jockey Club, the Union Club, the University Club, and the Union League Club of New York, all have private dining and reading rooms for the accommodation of their members only at the Manhattan Hotel. At the Brighton Hotel, the Bullion Club of New York, and the New York Club have similar quarters.

Compass.—*See* article on SUMMER STARS (POLE STAR) *in Appendix.*

Concourse (The)—[Map, I–J4]—is the wide asphalt drive and walk connecting West Brighton and Brighton Beaches. It is a smooth hard roadway about half a mile in length, and is intersected by the Ocean Parkway. Park wagons are constantly traversing it, fare five cents. It is maintained by the City of Brooklyn, and no buildings are permitted between it and the ocean. Two rustic cottages have been erected on the water side near the centre as a resting-place for promenaders.

Coney Island.—Some persons hold that this name was derived from the number of rabbits or conies which originally populated the island, others that it came from one Coneynen, an early Dutch settler, and a few that it is a corruption of Coleman, one of Hendrik Hudson's men who was murdered here. The former is probably the correct opinion, as the island, at the time of its discovery over 270 years ago, was hilly, covered with stunted cedar trees, beach plums and grape-vines, and populous with rabbits. The water-line at that time is supposed to have been two or three miles farther seaward than it is at present. *See also* HISTORY and GEOGRAPHY.

Coney Island in One Day.—*See* HOW TO SEE.

Coney Island Trip.—*See* TRIP TO.

Coney Island Creek, so called, is an arm of the sea, or a tidal channel flowing through salt marshes, dividing Coney Island from the main-land on the north, and joining the waters of Gravesend and Sheepshead Bays. There is good bass fishing to be had in the Creek. *See* FISH-ING.

Coney Island Jockey Club was incorporated June, 1879, by a number of gentlemen who are prominent in the American Jockey Club and sporting matters generally. Leonard W. Jerome is the president, and J. G. K. Lawrence sec-retary. The New York office of the Club is at No. 25 East 26th St. The race course, opened in June, 1880, for the spring meeting, is situated north of the Manhattan Hotel, across the head of Sheeps-head Bay, fronts on Ocean Avenue, and the grounds comprise 112 acres of fine sandy loam soil. It is three quarters of a mile from the beach; the N. Y. and Manhattan Railroad runs within 200 yards of it; the Brooklyn, Flatbush and Coney Island (Brighton Beach) Railroad within 400 yards; the Ocean Parkway is within a square of it, and a branch of the Marine Railway runs from Manhat-tan Beach across a bridge built across the bay almost to its gates. There is an elaborate entrance, a Grand Stand, weighing offices, saddling sheds, judges' stand, timers' stand, and music stand.

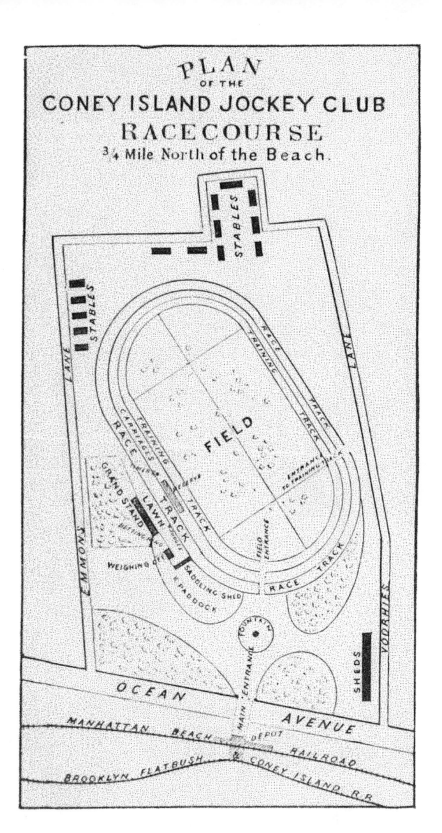

These buildings and the disposition of the en-
closed space will be found on the diagram. The
buildings are all picturesque structures in the
modified Queen Anne style of architecture, and the
whole aspect of the place charming. Two meet-
ings of six days each are held in June and September, at which selling races, sweepstakes, steeple
chases, and hurdle races are given. Among the
events, the Coney Island Derby and the Coney
Island Cup are likely to become famous. The
best stables in the country are represented, and
good racing may always be expected. The club
intends building a new club house in the Queen
Anne style adjoining the Manhattan Hotel, where
they now have temporary quarters. The initiation fee is $50 and the annual dues $25, but members of the American and Maryland Jockey Clubs
do not pay initiation fees. The capital stock of
the club is $250,000, most of it invested in the
lands and buildings of the association. Admission to the course during the race-meetings is as
follows. To tne Field, 50 cents; Field and
Open Stand, $1; Grand Stand and everywhere,
$2.50; Lady's Ticket, all privileges, $1; A badge
entitling the wearer to all privileges during the
six days of the meeting, may by purchased for $12.

Conterno's Band.—*See* WEST BRIGHTON BEACH
HOTEL.

Cow (Mechanical).—*See* PLAZA.

Cramp.—*See* article on SWIMMING, *in Appendix.*

Croquet.—Good grounds and the implements
of this game will be found at Brighton Beach and
at Paul Bauer's West Brighton Beach Hotel, adjoining the Plaza. The use of the grounds and
implements is charged for at moderate rates.

Culver's.—West Brighton Beach was formerly

known as Culver's Beach, and even now, the
Prospect Park and Coney Island Railroad is
called "Culver's Road," after its President, Mr.
Andrew R. Culver, who was the first to discover
the possibilities of Coney Island as a summer
resort, and to open it up to the public.

Dancing.—At Feltmann's Hotel at West Brighton there is a large dancing hall where dancing is
kept up from 2 to 11 P.M. The admission is
twenty-five cents for men, but women are admitted free. The place is a resort mainly for Germans of the middle class, and although there is a
total lack of ceremony, there is no rudeness or
disorder met with in the " ball-room."

Dangers.—*See* articles on BATHING and SWIM-
MING (Cautionary), *in Appendix.*

Dieter's [Map I–J4] is an ornamental frame
building near Ocean Parkway, and in the rear of
the Concourse. It is a restaurant, kept by one
Dieter, a well-known Brooklyn caterer, and is
patronized principally by persons driving down
from Brooklyn.

Dinners.—" To dine well at a moderate cost,"
says " Appletons' Dictonary of New York," " is
an art not to be taught in books, albeit much has
been written on the subject. To select from a
long and varied bill of fare those dishes which har-
monize, and each of which accents and enchances
the enjoyment to be derived from the others, re-
quires a taste both instinctive and acquired. Two
men may enter a restaurant where the cooking is
unexceptionable and the service perfect, and
order their dinners. It is not unlikely that the
one will dine badly off a villainous collection of
viands, each perfect in its way, while the other will

dine well at half the cost, from his superior taste and knowledge of the gastronomic art."

All that can be done here is to indicate the special features of Coney Island dinners and to leave the hungry man to his own resources and to his digestion. Remember, first, that at all restaurants of the better class one portion of any dish is ample for two persons, and in order to avoid any mistake write " one portion " on your order. A reference to " Restaurants " elsewhere will indicate the fact that the variation in restaurant prices at Coney Island is so small that you may select any restaurant in which to dine irrespective of that consideration, and, where the appearance of the dining-room and service attract you, enter in. If, however, chance or other circumstances lead you into one of the lower-class restaurants, you will fare best by confining yourself to clams and fish which they cook fairly well everywhere on the beach, and by carefully avoiding their entrées, etc. Many persons will find that they can dine more cheaply and better by patronizing the *table-d'hôte* dinners at a fixed price. (*See* TABLE-D'HÔTE DINNERS.)

A mistaken idea prevails among many people that two persons cannot dine at one of the first-class hotels without the expenditure of anywhere from five to ten dollars. The best way perhaps to indicate the folly of this will be to print one or two menus for a modest dinner, with the prices.

Dinner for two persons at Manhattan Beach Hotel.

Little Neck clams raw, 2 portions		.........$0	50
Soup Bisque of Crabs,	1	"	40
Baked Bluefish,	1	"	45
Mashed Potatoes,	1	··	10

Roast Lamb,	1 portion..........	60
Green Peas,	1 "	20
Lettuce Salad,	"	25
Meringue Glacée,	1 "	30
Coffee,	2 cups.............	20

Total.....................$3 00

The same dinner at the Brighton Beach Hotel would cost $2.70, or ten per cent less. Wine or beer is of course at discretion, and costs about the same as at New York hotels of the same grade.

Many persons would find their appetite satisfied before reaching the end of the menu given above or a similar number of courses, and the following will prove a guide for such :

Dinner for two persons at Brighton Beach Hotel.

Consommé Soup, 1 portion..............$0	25
Boiled Sheepshead, Sauce Hollandaise,	
1 portion (includes Potatoes)............	60
Roast Ribs of beef, 1 portion..	40
String-Beans, 1 "	20
Coffee, 2 cups..............	20

Total........................$1 65

This will prove ample for two persons with ordinary appetites, and at the Manhattan Hotel would cost say $1.80.

It will be apparent at once that these combinations of viands may be varied almost indefinitely, added to or omitted, but with the exercise of a little taste and discretion two persons can dine well at any restaurant on the beach for from $2 to $3, without wine, and by patronizing a *table-d'hôte* that may be had included for the same price. (*See also* FISH DINNERS ; CLAMBAKES; RESTAURANTS ; LOBSTERS ; FEES.)

Donkeys.—A drove of small donkeys will be found near the Concourse, in the Plaza at West Brighton Beach. They may be rented for a small sum for the use of children, and are always attended by a boy driver.

Drug Stores— The principal drug stores on the island are in small pavilions in the plaza at West Brighton, in front of the Brighton Hotel, and in front of the Manhattan Hotel. Prices are about the same as at first-class drug stores in New York.

Ebb.—*See* HIGH WATER.

Electric Lights are in common use along the beach, and serve to illuminate the water for bathing purposes, and the grounds in front of the Manhattan and Brighton Hotels, the Iron Pier, and the Plaza at West Brighton. The light is very white and rather ghastly in its effects

Engeman's Hotel.—*See* OCEAN HOTEL.

Engeman's Pier is a wooden structure extending out over the ocean for a distance of three or four hundred feet. It is not intended as a landing place for steamers, but is used for restaurant purposes and for the accommodation of picnic parties who bring their own lunch and desire to supplement the same with beer, clams, etc.

Engeman's Race-Course [Map KL 3] is the name commonly applied to the Brighton Beach Fair Grounds Course, in the rear of Engeman's and the Brighton Beach Hotels. The track has been considerably improved during the past year. Three days of very fair racing are given every week during the season.

Express—O'Connor's Coney Island Express forwards packages to any part of the island at reasonable rates. The offices are at 7 Fulton

3

Street, 3 Hudson Street, 7 New Church Street, New York, and 13 Fulton Street, Brooklyn. Packages are delivered at and collected from all the principal hotels on the Beach.

Dodd's Express takes baggage from New York to Manhattan Beach, twice daily, al 50 cents per package.

Eyeglasses.—*See* PEDLERS.

Faintness.—*See* HINTS ON BATHING, *in Appendix.*

Fashions.—*See* SURF STYLES, *in Appendix.*

Fees.—It is not of course necessary to fee the waiters and attendants at Coney Island hotels any more than it is at any other hotel, and there can be no two opinions about the system being all wrong. Nevertheless it is one which exists, and a well-invested dime or quarter will frequently secure for you added comfort and attention quite out of proportion to the amount laid out. If you are a frequent visitor at any one restaurant or hotel on the island, and neglect to remember that the waiter "hath an itching palm," you will subsequently be made unpleasantly aware of your short-comings. If you are only a casual visitor, and do not expect to return soon, fees may as well be omitted.

Feltman's Hotel—[Map, H4]—is a large frame building at West Brighton Beach, which is largely patronized by the middle classes, and especially by Germans. There are large dining-rooms, bar-rooms, and lunch tables on the lower floor, and on the upper two large halls. One of these, 60 x 200 feet, is set apart for dancing, and music is provided for that purpose daily, from 2 to 11 P.M. Admission to this hall is fixed at 25 cents for men, but women are admitted free. The dancing is marked as much by vigor as by grace, and the prevailing etiquette elastic rather than rigid.

The second hall, erected this year, is 300 x 60, and is used as a theatre. There are billiard-tables and bowling to be had at this house. The prices are a trifle lower than at other hotels in the vicinity, and the cooking rather of the modern German school. Something over 200 bathrooms are attached to this hotel.,¹

Feltman's Theatre [Map, H4], built 1880, is in the second story of a frame building, adjoining his Hotel on the east (see Feltman's Hotel). It is under the direction of Prof. Seemann, of Berlin, who is what may be called a scientific wonder-worker. His performances not only include all the tricks of the ordinary magician, but he uses electrical instruments to assist him, and thereby is able to accomplish many very cunning changes. He uses an electro-motor for musical effects, engaging instruments that are affixed in different parts of the theatre. His daughter, Miss Seemann, floats in the air without the aid of any rod or pole and without any support whatever, certainly without any that is visible to the spectator upon closest inspection. He has dissolving views upon an entirely new principle, in which he produces water fountains, the jets of which spout water in many different colors. He will also produce on the screen the photograph in large size of any persons who choose to hand him their *cartes de visite* for that purpose.

Two born blind musicians also appear. One is a violinist named Schafer, of Bremen, who composes his own music. The other is a pianist, Werpach, a Swiss, claimed to be equal to Joseffy. He is also a performer on the cello. They appear in solos and duets. The performances are in English, and the price of admission is 25 cents.

Fireworks.—Exhibitions of fireworks are given at Manhattan, Brighton, and West Brighton Beaches, usually once a week at each place during the season. Advertisements in all the daily papers announce the exact dates of these events. A good way to see the fireworks to advantage is by taking the Rockaway boat down and back during the evening, and, passing along the Coney Island shore, view them from the steamer's deck.

Fish Dinners.—The one glory of the restaurants on Coney Island is that the best edibles they furnish, the cheaper as well as the most expensive, are fish and clams. At almost any place you may select, however rough the service, these articles of food are very sure to be well cooked, but as the prices are pretty much the same everywhere, it is as well to patronize a first-class house. At Manhattan Pavilion and at Point Breeze (which see) they make a specialty of fish dinners. Blue-fish, striped bass, sea bass, eels, flounders, weak-fish, sheepshead, Spanish mackerel, sole, black-fish, king-fish, and whitebait may all be had at the island, and preceded by a few Little Neck clams, you may eat whichever you like and as much as you like, and have them cooked to suit your taste. *See* CLAMBAKES, DINNERS and RESTAURANTS.

Fishing—The opportunities for good fishing in and about New York are not many, but among the best are those afforded at or near Coney Island. If you wish to troll for blue fish or Spanish mackerel there are capital grounds off Rockaway Beach, and your best plan is to go down to Point Breeze (*which see*), pass the night at the

Pavilion, and having made your arrangements for a sailboat (*see* ROWING, SAILING). crew, bait, lunch, etc., over night, make an early start in the morning. If you are after bass, you can find good fishing in Coney Island Creek and Sheepshead Bay, starting out from the Pavilion at Point Breeze ; or you may take the Prospect Park and Coney Island Railway to Van Sicklen's Station and stop at ' The" Alston's Hotel," where the rates for full board are from $2 to $3 per day, and fish in the Coney Island Creek. Rod and reel and crab bait are used If you meet with the proverbial " fisherman's luck," the fresh air and the capital " good cheer" obtainable at either of these places will well repay you for the trip.

Floating.—*See* article on SWIMMING, *in Appendix.*

Geography.—Coney Island is the extreme western end of a great outlying sand-bar, broken by inlets, which extend along the southern coast of Long Island for nearly ninety miles. Its dif ferent sections are known as Coney Island, Pelican, Rockaway, Hog, Long, Crow, Jones, Oak Island, Fire Island, and Great South beaches. Coney Island is bounded on the north by Gravesend Bay, Coney Island Creek, and Sheepshead Bay, and on the south by the Atlantic Ocean. It is divided on the east from Pelican Beach (or Barren Island) by Plumb Inlet, which connects Sheepshead Bay with the ocean. The western extremity of the island is known as Norton's Point, and the eastern extremity as Point Breeze. The island is subdivided into West End, West Brighton, Brighton and Manhattan Beaches, each of which will be found described elsewhere. The entire island is a sandy beach, devoid of any nat-

ural growth other than beach grass, and the main-
land to the north of Coney Island Creek is composed of extensive salt marshes. The island is
about eleven miles directly south of the city of
New York, although the distance from the Battery
to Norton's Point is only about eight and a half
miles as the bird flies. The average width of the
island is not above half a mile. (See also *History.*)

Gilmore's Band.—*See* MANHATTAN HOTEL.

Goggles.—*See* PEDLERS.

Grafulla's Band.—*See* IRON PIER.

Grand Central Hotel—[Map, J4]—is an
ornamental three-story frame building, surrounded with balconies on each floor, and ample facilities for the temporary care of horses and carriages. It is on Ocean Parkway, near its junc-
tion with the Concourse, and is frequently called
Bader's Hotel. There are about 40 rooms, nicely
furnished, hot and cold water on each floor, and
gas in every room. Rates for rooms from $2 to
$3 per day. The restaurant will accommodate
about 150 persons at one time, and the house is
a pleasant and attractive stopping-place.

Grand Union Hotel [Map I3] is back of the
Plaza at West Brighton, and east of the Depot of
the Brooklyn, Bath and Coney Island Railroad.
The Brooklyn horse-cars have their terminus at
the east end of the hotel. The building is three
stories high, plainly furnished, and contains
about 100 sleeping-rooms, which are rented at
from $2 to $3 per day. The house is also on the
American plan, and gives fair board at $3 per day,
or $15 to $20 per week. It is kept by A.
Chamberlain.

Gunther's Road.—*See* BROOKLYN, BATH AND
CONEY ISLAND RAILROAD.

Half-Way House—[Map, D4]—is a small frame building near the landing of the West End Pier. It has a bar and restaurant at cheap prices.

Headache.—*See* HINTS ON BATHING, *in Appendix.*

High Water.—The time chosen for bathing, says Dr. Durant, should immediately precede or coincide with that of high water, for then we have the advantage of easy access to the ocean and the least possible exposure in returning to the bath-house ; moreover, the water is then most free from the impurities which it contains at low tide.   Let us briefly explain why the tidal phenomena take place in the same way at two points upon the earth's surface which are diametrically opposed : What first attracts our attention is the ebb and flow of the waters.   These oscillations are periodical.   The water flows toward one portion of the earth during the space of six hours ; this constitutes the rising of the tide ; it then remains stationary for about fifteen minutes ; it is now called high water.   From this it begins to recede.   The time taken by the water to return to its lowest point is about the same as it occupied in rising to the highest ; this is termed low tide or full ebb.   After remaining at this point for a quarter of an hour, it again resumes its former motion, and so continues in its oscillations. During a lunar day (a space of twenty-four hours, fifty minutes—the time elapsing between the moon being over the meridian of her place and returning to it), the tides have changed twice. From this it follows that the tides are daily fifty minutes later, that is, if on a certain day at any place it be high water at 1 P.M., on the following day it will be high water at 1.50 P.M., the day after at 2.40 P.M., and so on."

History.—At first glance it might seem that the history of a sand-bank like Coney Island could scarcely present any features of special interest, but it does not require any great stretch of imagination or historical truth to connect the island with the discovery of New York. The story may be told best in the words of a little history of Manhattan Beach :

"About two hundred and seventy years ago (April, 1609), Hendrick Hudson, having sailed from Amsterdam in search of a Western path to the East Indies, stood off the shore of Coney Island. His little vessel, the *Halve Moene*, had for five months buffeted the storms and been driven from Greenland to the Carolinas, when, upon the 3d of September, he sighted 'three great rivers,' one of which was probably the Hudson, the other Raritan Bay and the third Rockaway Inlet. On the day following, according to his journal, he sent a number of his men ashore in a boat, 'who caught ten great mullet and a ray, as great as four men could haul into the ship.' They found large numbers of plum-trees loaded with fruit and surrounded by luxuriant grape-vines. The natives who came to meet them were astonished at the size of their ship, and vastly interested in their dress, language and color. Hudson's intercourse with the Indians was amicable in the beginning, they came on board his ship and traded tobacco, maize and fruit for knives and beads ; but on the third day, whilst some of the sailors were ashore, the savages—probably not without provocation— attacked them. John Coleman was killed by an arrow wound in the throat, and two others were wounded. Hudson then moved his ship to an anchorage in Gravesend Bay, which is bounded on the southwest by the western extremity of the island."

The island forms a part of the township of Gravesend, which was settled in 1635 by a few English colonists, including a number of Quakers who had been expelled from the neighborhood of Boston, among them Lady Deborah Moody, who exercised a great influence on the affairs of the colony. In 1699' a ship was built, measuring about seventy tons, and during the war of Independence, an English corvette of twenty guns was captured off Coney Island. Gravesend Bay was also the scene of General Howe's landing, as he removed his forces from Staten Island to Long Island, previous to the battle on the Heights.

Gen. Howe quartered his troops on the villagers and compelled the men to work on the fortifications. The corvette referred to anchored late one night off Coney Island, whence she was bound to Halifax, and a gallant old whaler named Huyler, smarting perhaps under the wrongs suffered at the hands of the red-coats, conceived the bold idea of seizing and destroying her. A few trusty friends coöperated with him in the exploit ; they muffled their oars and rowed under the stern of the ship ; no watch was on deck, and the officers could be seen through the cabin windows playing a game of cards. A second boat stood some dis tance behind the first, and at a signal one crew boarded the corvette over the port side and the other over the starboard. Both officers and men were completely surprised and taken at a disadvantage, were soon overpowered, bound, and lowered into the boats. The corvette was then set on fire and the captors pulled over to the Jersey shore with their prisoners.

The captain of the corvette is said to have wept bitterly, whether from the mellowing effects of wine or chagrin is not known. "To be surprised and taken by two d——d eggshells is too bad," he complained.

He praised the gallantry and enterprise of Huyler, however, and told him that there were forty thousand dollars on board the ship that was illuminating the whole bay with its flames; but the treasure was not secured.

During the following years Coney Island was little more than a desolate sand-heap. The wind played havoc with the shifting sands, and swept away the cedars and the grape-vines. A few " clammers " and oystermen inhabited huts along the creek, and now and then a sportsman came in winter after game. Meantime a city rivalling in many respects the capitals of the Old World grew up almost within sight of the beach. Not many years ago a few hotels and restaurants sprang up at the West End, but these attracted only the lower and the criminal classes. The excursion steamers by which the beach was reached, were overcrowded, and the ruffianly conduct of their passengers and the indecorous scenes on the beach gave the island a bad name. A horse-car route from Fulton Ferry, then a steam railway from near Greenwood Cemetery came into existence, but it was not until 1874 that the island attracted any attention as a resort for respectable people. In June, 1874, Mr. Andrew Culver, President, opened the Prospect Park and Coney Island Railway. The project had been jeered at and its failure predicted by every one, but Mr. Culver pushed the work to completion almost unaided, and the result justified his faith. From that time Coney Island became the objective point of thousands of excursionists, and the character of the place correspondingly improved. The "three-card monte" men, gamblers, confidence men and thieves were driven away by the police, and good order maintained everywhere. In 1875, a new hotel was built, and in 1877 the Manhattan Beach Hotel and Railway were thrown open to the public. At present this magnificent stretch of beach, almost at the very doors of the metropolis, but neglected for a century, is fulfilling its mission as the greatest seaside resort in the world.

Hotels.—Every shed on the Coney Island beach is dignified by the name of hotel, although not more than one half of them have any sleeping-rooms attached. In all there are about fifty so-called hotels scattered along the shore, between Norton's Point and Point Breeze, and these are of varying degrees of merit and respectability. At the west end there are a host of small resorts little better than shanties, which have not been deemed worthy of mention in this work, and these are the gathering places of a class of people, of both sexes. whom it is just as well to avoid. The most important of the west end resorts will, however, be found on the accompanying map, and are referred to briefly under their respective titles. At West Brighton there are good ·hotels of the type common to seaside resorts, and of varying degrees of excellence, which cater to different nationalities and classes—Feltman's and Bauer's, for example, being largely frequented by Germans, and Cable's being kept, except the restaurant, exclusively for the male sex. At the east end, however, there are three hotels which exceed in size and in the elegance of their appointments any watering-place hotels in the world. The Brighton and Manhattan are largely devoted to the comfort of transient visitors, and the Oriental to the wants of families who are permanent guests. Gas and running water, superb furniture and decorations, unequalled service, and a splendid cuisine are afforded by them at prices proportioned to these accommodations.

Almost all of the hotels are kept on the European plan, but at some few you may elect to remain on the American or European plan at dis cretion. This latter is the case at the Brighton Hotel and at the plainer houses, such as the Grand Union and Oceanic at West Brighton. As to prices, the range is not proportioned to the variations in the character of the accommodation. At Cable's Hotel gentlemen may secure rooms, without board, at $1 per day, but this is the brilliant exception to the rule that at all of the better class of houses the lowest price per day for a single room is $2; and per week, $12. Starting from this rate as a minimum rooms may be had at the Oriental and the other east end hotels as high as $10 or even $15 per day. For full board, $3 per day or $15 per week may be stated as the lowest rate, and at the Brighton $5 per day is the standard rate. At Manhattan Beach both hotels are strictly on the European plan. The following is a complete list of the principal hotels, arranged alphabetically, and a description of each will be found under its appropriate head (*See also* RESTAURANTS) :

Brighton Hotel.	Norton & Murray's Pavilion.
Dieter's Restaurant.	Ocean Concourse Hotel.
Grand Central Hotel.	Ocean Hotel.
Grand Union Hotel.	Oceanic Hotel.
Half-way House.	Oriental Hotel.
Leach's West End Hotel.	Point Breeze Pavilion.
Manhattan Hotel.	Point Comfort House.

Ravenhall.
Rosedale House.
St. Nicholas Hotel.
Sea Beach Hotel.
Sleight's Pavilion.

Smith's (Mrs.) Hotel.
Surf House.
Ward's Hotel.
West Brighton Beach Hotel.
Windsor Hotel.

How to See Coney Island in One Day.— The following directions are, with few exceptions, from Appleton's Dictionary of New York :

For the stranger who may desire to visit the whole island in one day, the following schedule will serve as a guide : Leave New York from the foot of West 24th Street, West 10th Street, Franklin Street, or Pier No. 2 adjoining the Battery, by steamer, passing Governor's Island, the Narrows, Forts Wadsworth, Tompkins, and Lafayette, and arriving at Norton's dock in an hour. Fare, twenty-five cents. Do not purchase a return ticket. These boats leave about every hour, and it is well in taking this trip to start not later than noon. Walk up to Norton's Hotel. Take the railroad to West Brighton ; fare, ten cents. See the plaza, the new pier, the camera-obscura (ten cents), and the great cow, ascend to the top of the observatory (fifteen cents), and then lunch at one of the neighboring hotels. Take a park wagon at Vanderveer's (five cents), and ride over the Concourse to Brighton. See the hotel and grounds, visit the pavilion and bathing-grounds, walk the length of the short pier at Engeman's, and then take the Marine Railway (five cents) to Manhattan Beach. See the hotel and grounds, and then bathe. The charge for bath-house and dress is twenty-five cents, including the care and guarrantee of valuables ; no reduction is made to those who take their own dresses. After or before the bath visit the amphitheatre overlooking the bathing-grounds (no charge to bathers for admission, ten cents to others). Then visit the Oriental Hotel, and take the Marine Railway (ten cents) to Point Breeze and return. Dine at Manhattan Beach or Brighton Beach. Hear the concert in the evening, see the effect of the electric light on the water, and return to New York at ten o'clock via Manhattan Beach road (fare thirty-five cents), landing at the foot of East 23d Street. This trip involves a considerable outlay of strength. The cost for two persons, including a modest dinner and lunch, is not more than $6 ; for one person it would be about $4. This includes all the sights, and may be considerably modified if desirable.

Iron Pier — [Map, H4–5]—This remarkable structure was erected by the Ocean Navigation and Pier Co. in the spring of 1879, and projects into the ocean from a point at the west side of the Plaza at West Brighton. The pier is built on 260 tubular iron piles, 9 inches in diameter, sunk in the sand to a depth of from 15 to 20 feet, and well braced by a system of horizontal struts and rods. It extends into the ocean at right angles with the shore for a distance of 1000 feet, and its general width is 50 feet, with enlargements to 120 feet at the shore end, 83 feet 4 inches at the centre, and 100 feet at the pier head. The entire structure is elevated above all possible reach of storm waves, and has two decks, an upper or promenade and a lower or main deck. An ornamental iron roof covers the upper deck, and at the widest points picturesque-looking buildings have been erected. The depth of water at the end of the pier is 18 feet, and an exterior row of oak fender piles surrounds the pier head to facilitate the landing of steamers. The flooring is of yellow pine, an ornamental iron railing surrounds it, and the whole furnishes a splendid promenade, day and night. A row of iron aquaria are placed along the upper deck, and a band-stand, where promenade music is furnished during the afternoon and evening by Grafulla's band. A restaurant on this deck is capable of feeding 1500 persons at one time and cigar and refreshment-stands and bar will also be found here. An excellent table d'hote dinner with wine is served daily at $1 per head, (including wine). The price of admission to the pier is 10 cents for each person, but those going to or from the Island by steamers landing at this pier, are furnished with coupons of admission on purchasing their tickets. On the lower deck are the bathing-houses and the ladies' parlor and retiring-rooms. It is lighted at night by powerful electric lights. The appearance of the pier, gayly decked with bunting, covered with people by, day and twinkling with lights at night, is very attractive, and it is well worth a visit.

Iron Pier, Bathing.—On the main or lower deck of the iron pier are placed 1200 bathing houses of excellent quality, with commodious offices and parlors attached. These baths have the unique advantage of being situated directly over the ocean, which is reached by two iron stair cases. The one nearest the shore leads down into the surf, where a good supply of life lines and other safeguards are located ; and the other leads down to the smooth water beyond the line of breakers, and affords a splendid opportunity for a good swim without buffeting the surf. At the head of each staircase is a shower of fresh water, which bathers can use on emerging from their bath. Valuables are taken care of by the check system, and this service is included in the charge

of twenty-five cents for a bath. There is a ladies'
hairdressing saloon attached to the bath in charge
of experienced operators. You may leave your
own bathing suit here for $1 per annum.

Ladies' Hairdressing Saloons are attached to
the principal bathing pavilions.

Land Breezes and Mosquitoes.—Perhaps the
most unpleasant phase of the weather at the seashore, says Dr. Packard, is experienced when
a land breeze prevails for several days ; the heat
may then be intense, and occasionally continues
throughout the nights as well as during the daytime. Late in the summer, and through the early
autumn, such a breeze brings hosts of mosquitoes,
which add greatly to the annoyance due to the
heat. Any strong odor will keep the mosquitoes
off; eau de cologne, bay-rum, or spirits of cam-
phor may be used to bathe the face and hands
occasionally. To allay the irritation caused by
their stings—strictly speaking, they do not bite—
the best remedy is strong spirits of hartshorn or
ammonia directly applied.

Leach's West End Hotel [Map F4] is a
small house west of the Surf House, and is conducted for the plainer class at cheap rates.

Levy, Cornet-Soloist, plays at the MANHATTAN
HOTEL (which *see*).

Life-Saving Station. [Map P4].—A little to
the east of the new Oriental Hotel is one of the
life-saving stations of the United States, which is
unoccupied, however, from May until November.
During the winter months the beach is patrolled
nightly by the surf-men attached to the station.
Each patrolman carries a beach lantern and a red
Coston hand-light, and on the discovery of a vessel in distress, he burns the latter, both to alarm

his companions and to give notice to those on the
wreck that succor is near. A life-boat, life-car,
mortar and shell, rockets and the other life-saving paraphernalia are then brought from the station to the spot thus indicated.

Livery Stable—[Map, I3–4]—will be found in
a building formerly used as a variety theatre,
north-east of the plaza at West Brighton.

Lobsters.—A delicious lunch may be made of
lobster without fear of indigestion by complying
with the following rules : Order the waiter at any
good restaurant to bring you a small lobster, or
half a large one in the shell, a lemon, a raw egg,
and olive oil, red pepper, and a soup-plate.
Separate the yolk from the white of the egg, drop
it into the soup-plate, and stir it with a fork
(always stir one way), and slowly add olive oil
until the mixture is of the consistency of dough,
and will drop from the fork, then add a portion of
red pepper about the size of half a pea, a pinch of
salt, and the juice of a small lemon, or a half a
large one. This will reduce the dressing to the
consistency of cream. Then pick the meat of the
lobster from the shell, tearing it with a silver
fork, but on no account cutting or touching it
with a knife, add some few leaves of fresh crisp
lettuce torn in pieces with the fingers, and pour
the dressing over it. Eat with dry French bread.
This will be found the perfection of æsthetic
eating.

Lost and Found.—Lost children or lost articles
of value should at once be reported to the police
office in the Aquarium. (*See* POLICE.)

Low Tide.—*See* HIGH WATER.

Lunch.—*See* DINNERS.

4

Lunch Tables.—*See* PICNICS.

Manhattan Beach is the name given to all that portion of the Island lying east of Brighton Beach, and extending to Point Breeze, the eastern extremity of the Island. It has an uninterrupted sea front of over 2½ miles, and embraces some 500 acres. It is the property of the Manhattan Beach Improvement Company, which owns in fee simple the entire tract. The buildings erected by the company up to the present time (1880), comprise the Manhattan Hotel, opened in 1877, and the railroad depot adjoining it in the rear, also necessary out-buildings ; the Oriental Hotel, erected 1880 ; the Manhattan Beach Bathing Pavilion and Amphitheatre, a grand pavilion, and a small house at Point Breeze. Depots of the Marine Railway, a drug store, and the music-stand complete the list. Next year a superb specimen of Queen Anne architecture will be erected west of the Manhattan Hotel by the Coney Island Jockey Club.

Manhattan Beach Bathing Pavilion [Map N4] is east of the Manhattan Hotel, and including the Amphitheatre is 520 feet long by 170 feet deep. The building is an ornamental but substantial frame structure, two stories high, and the interior is finished in natural woods. The entrances to the bathing-houses are in the rear, and the sexes separate on the beach, the ladies' door being at the right and the gentlemen's at the left. The bather purchases a ticket, as a primary step, for 25 cents, which entitles him to the use of a bathing-suit, a bathing-house and the care of his valuables without restriction as to time. The parlors and offices are handsomely furnished, and it is well to leave your valuables at the desk. These you place in an envelope which is handed you, seal up and write your name across the flap. An attendant then gives you a numbered check strung on a rubber cord, which you hang about your neck while in the water. The presentation of this check and the signing of your name in a register will secure the return of your valuables, after the signature on the envelope has been compared with that on the register and found to correspond. This is a perfect check, and losses are unknown. There are about 2200 bathing-houses in all, 800 of which are for ladies. The men's rooms are 4 feet x 4 feet, and contain a fixed seat, a foot-tub, a mirror, shelf-hooks, two towels, and running fresh water. The ladies' rooms are 4 feet 6 inches x 6 feet in length, but in all other respects are like those described. The entire stretch of beach in front of the bath-house is reserved for bathers, is carefully fenced in, and a space of 50 feet is set apart for ladies exclusively. There are a plentiful supply of life-lines, floats beyond the line of breakers afford places for experienced swimmers to dive from, and a life-boat manned by experienced seamen is kept constantly in the water, and another is ready upon the beach for use in case of accident.

Two policemen are always on duty at this point, and accidents or disturbances are unknown. The beach is kept scrupulously clean, and at night is illuminated by a powerful electric light. Should you prefer you may take your own bathing-suit to the place, and on payment of $1 hire a box for the season in which to keep it. It will only be delivered to you on presentation of your box ticket, and it is carefully washed and dried each time it is used, without extra charge, and returned to your address by express at the close of the season, or stored during the winter, without charge, as you may elect. This is by far the best plan. The bathing-suits furnished, however, are of good quality, of flannel if you prefer it, and washed and dried by steam each time they are used. Over the parlors are 150 private bath-rooms, where hot and cold and shower baths may be had by those who do not care for surf bathing. The charge for these baths is 50 cents. (*See also* AMPHITHEATRE.)

Manhattan Beach Railroad.—*See* NEW YORK AND MANHATTAN BEACH RAILROAD.

Manhattan Hotel [Map N4] is, with one exception, the largest of its kind in the world. It was first opened to the public in 1877. Standing within 400 feet of the ocean at high tide, it has a frontage of 660 feet, is alternately three and four stories in height, and is a picturesque-looking building, having a marvellously light and airy appearance for so huge a structure. A wide-covered balcony surrounds it on three sides, and the depot of the New York and Manhattan Beach Railway Company is directly in the rear. A wide plaza in front, laid out with grass-plots, flower-beds and shrubbery extends nearly to the water's edge, and the broad plank walks by which it is intersected converge at the music stand directly in front of the hotel. At this stand Gilmore's Twenty-second Regiment Band give concerts daily at 3.30 P.M. and at 7 P.M., and another band plays during the day in the Amphitheatre of the Bathing Pavilion.

The hotel contains 360 sleeping-rooms, all of which are light and airy, finished in natural wood, handsomely carpeted and furnished with Eastlake furniture. These rooms are rented at from $2 to $4 per day, and for suites of rooms proportionately higher rates are charged. Persons desiring to engage rooms for a whole or a part of the season can obtain a slight discount from these rates. Permanent guests are provided with parlors, dining-rooms, etc., on the second floor, to which transient guests are not admitted, " transient guests" being used here to designate excursionists who do not remain over night. The first floor is, however, free to all well-behaved persons, and the use of the rooms does not imply any obligation either to eat, drink, or in any way patronize the house. Meals are served in a grand dining-room in the west wing of the hotel, which is capable of seating over a thousand persons, and there are two other public and several small dining, rooms, in addition to the piazzas, where meals for four thousand persons can be served at one time, and 30,000 persons fed in one day. The cuisine is unexceptionable (*see* RESTAURANTS), and the prices are in proportion. Bar-rooms will be found in the east wing, but there are no billiard-tables or bowling-alleys in the hotel. The Union Club, Union League Club, University Club of New York, and the Coney Island Jockey Club all have seaside branches of their clubs located in private suites of apartments (used as dining, smoking, and reading rooms) in the Manhattan Hotel. There is gas in every room, and a good supply of hot and cold water and comfortable retiring-rooms for both sexes in every part of the hotel. Further information will be found under RESTAURANTS, MUSIC, and BATHING.

Manhattan Pavilion [Map, N4] stands to the east of the Manhattan Hotel, and is designed especially for the use of excursionists, and particularly for picnic parties. It is an enormous structure, fitted with an abundance of tables and chairs and waiters, for the free use of the public. There is a bar, cigar and lunch counters in the main hallway, and a restaurant supplies chowder,

fish, and clams, and beer or wine to those who
desire to supplement with any of these things
the lunches with which they have provided themselves. (*See* PIC-NICS.)

Marine Railways.—There are two so-called
marine railways on Coney Island, which together
extend the whole length of the Island, with the exception of a break of half a mile between the plaza
at West Brighton and Brighton Beach. The road
at the west end is a branch of the Prospect Park
and Coney Island Railway, and starts from a
point near Norton's dock at the west end, and runs
along parallel with the shore, but in the rear of the
hotels, to the P. P. & C. I. R. R. Depot at West
Brighton. There is a station at a point midway
between the termini at Rosedale. The road at the
west end is a branch of the New York and Manhattan Beach Railway, and starts from a station
near the east end of the Brighton Beach Bathing
Pavilion and runs to Manhattan Beach. From
the rear of the Manhattan and Oriental Hotels, it
continues on to Point Breeze. Near the Manhattan Hotel a branch of this road is to be built
northward across Sheepshead Bay on piles to the
race-course of the Coney Island Jockey Club.
The fare on either road is 5 cents for the whole
trip or between any two points.

Mechanical Cow.—*See* PLAZA.

Midgets' Palace [Map L4] is in the Brighton
Beach Bathing Pavilion, and is a large hall capable of holding about 700 persons. The curious
little people called the "Midgets" are on exhibi-
tion here from 11 A.M. to 10 P.M., supplemented
by the Lilliputian Opera Company. The admission is fixed at 10 cents.

Milk.—*See* description of Mechanical Cow, under heading PLAZA.

Moonlight-nights.—*See* CALENDAR, *in Appendix.*

Mosquitoes.—(*See* LAND BREEZES.)

Music.—One of the greatest attractions at Coney Island is found in the music furnished, much of which is of a high order of merit, although, like almost everything else on the island, you may have the best or the worst. All of the best orchestras and military bands of New York are engaged by the principal hotels, and every afternoon and evening excellent programmes of popular music are rendered for the gratuitous delectation of the visitors. At Manhattan Beach the music is furnished by the Twenty-second Regiment Band, under the leadership of P. S. Gilmore, and the soloists are Jules Levy, the unrivalled cornet-soloist, and Signor Raffayello, who performs on a novel and complex instrument, called the euphonium-trombone. A good band also plays in the Amphitheatre adjoining the bathing-pavilion. At Brighton Beach Ad. Neuendorf and his fine orchestra furnish the music, and at Cable's Downing's Ninth Regiment Band and Arbuckle, the cornet-soloist, may be heard daily. Carlberg's Orchestra furnish the visitors at the Sea Beach Hotel with music. Graffula's famous Seventh Regiment Band are stationed on the Iron Pier, Conterno's Twenty-third Regiment band at Bauer's Hotel, and the Sixth Regiment Band at Feltman's. From strolling musicians and musical organizations of all kinds are drawn the forces of the minor hotels, but at almost every place, from land's end to land's end, may be heard the twanging of harps and the squeaking of fiddles, while at intervals the steam-orchestrion at the Aquarium drowns every sound for half a mile around.

Nausea.—*See* HINTS ON BATHING, *in Appendix.*

Neuendorf's Orchestra.—*See* BRIGHTON HOTEL.

New York and Manhattan Beach Railroad runs from Greenpoint and from Bay Ridge to the Manhattan Hotel over a narrow gauge steel rail double track. Between Bay Ridge and the Beach it runs through cool, charming woodlands for a good portion of the distance. Connections with New York are made by steamers from points on the North River running to Bay Ridge and by boats from the foot of East 23d Street to Greenpoint. The Woodruff Palace Cars are run on this road and are models of luxury and convenience, affording the shelter needed by fastidious persons, invalids and others from dust and draughts. The extra fare is 25 cents.

☞ *See* TIME-TABLE *in Appendix.*

New York and Sea Beach Railroad runs from Third Avenue and 65th Street, Brooklyn (Bay Ridge) to the depot at West Brighton Beach. The Bay Ridge depot is accessible by horse-cars from Fulton Ferry *via* Court Street, and from Hamilton Ferry *via* Fort Hamilton horse-cars. From New York it is reached by steamers to Bay Ridge.

☞ *See* TIME-TABLE *in Appendix.*

Norton and Murray's Pavilion—[Map, A-B3] —is located about a quarter of a mile south-east of the steamboat dock at Norton's Point, and is reached by a wide plank walk. The pavilion comprises three buildings, all of them old and somewhat rude structures. The largest building contains some 700 bath houses of the old-fashioned type, simply rude unfurnished cabins. The centre building is the pavilion proper, and contains a bar and restaurant. The third building to the west-ward is a small shanty bearing the sign "Coney Island Stock Exchange," and there is an office of the WESTERN UNION TELEGRAPH COMPANY in it, and tables for the use of picnic parties who bring their lunch with them. During the season this place is largely patronized, chiefly, however, by the middle and lower classes, and undoubtedly it furnishes them with amusement and recreation quite to their taste.

Norton's Dock—[Map, A1]—is a rough wooden pier, about 150 feet long, at the extreme west end of the Island, and has been the landing place of the Coney Island boats for many years. It is at the mouth of Gravesend Bay, and is sheltered from the extreme force of the wind and waves, and landings are readily made in any but extraordinarily heavy weather. Norton & Murray's Hotel (Pavilion) is near the shore end of the pier and the depot of the Brooklyn, Bath and Coney Island Railway, by which West Brighton Beach can be reached in a few minutes.

Norton's Point [Map, A1]—is the extreme western end of the Island, and takes its name from ex-Senator Mike Norton, proprietor of a hotel at that place. It has Gravesend Bay on the north and the Atlantic Ocean on the south. The old steamboat dock is at this point, and a depot of the Prospect Park and Coney Island Railway, by which it is connected with West Brighton. The sand on the beach roundabout is heaped up by the wind in a series of irregular and ever shifting hillocks or sand-dunes;

beach grass grows in ragged tufts here and
there ; the beach is partially covered with seaweed, and its general aspect desolate and un-
inviting. It was however, one of the first places
of resort on the Island, and five or six years
ago attracted many visitors from among the
lower classes, and was made notorious by the
gamblers and blacklegs who infested the beach.
This has all been changed, and the beach at this
point, if not attractive, is quiet and orderly.

Observatory (The). — [Map, H4]—A tower
whose skeleton frame stretches up 300 feet into
the air, occupies a prominent place near the centre
of the plaza at West Brighton, and is called the
Observatory. The top is reached by the same large
elevators which were in use at the Philadelphia
Exposition in 1876. A superb view of the harbor
and bay of New York and their islands, the Jersey
coast and Sandy Hook, portions of Long Island,
the Hudson River, and the adjacent cities, is
afforded those who make the ascent. The charge
is fifteen cents for adults and ten cents for children.

Ocean Concourse Hotel—[Map, I4]—is at the
north-east corner of the plaza at West Brighton,
and is a favorite resort for persons driving down
from Brooklyn. It is one of the oldest and best
known places on the Island, and has spacious
sheds for the temporary accommodation of vehi-
cles. The hotel contains 50 rooms, rented at $2
per day and $10 to $15 a week each. The dining-
rooms and piazza will accommodate about 200
persons at table at one time ; the service is good,
and the food well cooked (*see* RESTAURANTS).
There is a billiard room and bar room in the
house. The baths are in a small building in front,
which also contains a bar and restaurant (*see*

BATHING). The house is frequently called Vanderveer's, that being the name of the proprietor.

Ocean Hotel [Map, K4]—is a few rods west of the Brighton Beach Hotel, near the Concourse, and is a medium size frame building, two stories in height, surrounded by a spacious veranda. It contains about 20 sleeping apartments, which are rented at $12 per week or $2 per day, without board. The restaurant is neat and attractive looking, and the food of excellent quality (*see* RESTAURANTS). It is kept by Wm. A. Engeman, who also owns a wooden pier (*see* ENGEMAN'S PIER), which is almost directly in front of the hotel.

Ocean Parkway.—A broad and straight roadway or boulevard, 5½ miles in length, leading in a direct course from Prospect Park to Coney Island, striking the beach midway on the Ocean Concourse, about half a mile west of Brighton Hotel. The main roadway is 200 feet wide, macadamized and bordered with shade-trees. A sidewalk, partially flagged, is at either side of the main roadway, and beyond these walks are extra roadways, each twenty-five feet wide. Taken in connection with the drive through Prospect Park and along the Ocean Concourse this combined drive of 8½ miles is almost unrivalled for attractiveness and pleasure.

Ocean View Hotel [Map H3], faces the Plaza at West Brighton Beach and adjoins the depot of the Prospect Park and Coney Island Railroad. It is kept by Thomas E. Cable and is commonly called "Cable's." It is a plain two-story building, with a wide piazza around the two stories, and meals are served on these and in the front dining-room below. The upper balcony is a

pleasant place to eat, and the panorama to be
seen is very picturesque. A billiard and bar-
room will be found on the first floor in the rear.
There are about sixty sleeping-rooms in the
house, which are rented at $1 per day each, to
gentlemen only. This is an inflexible rule. The
restaurant is one of the best on this part of the
Island.

Oceanic Hotel [Map I2] is situated some
distance back from the beach, and is quiet and
secluded. The house contains about 100 rooms,
and is plainly furnished. The board rates are
from $2 to $3 per day, and families are accommo-
dated for the season at moderate rates.

O'Connor's Express.—*See* Express.

Oriental Hotel [Map, O4] was erected during the present season (1880) by the Manhattan
Beach Improvement Company, to supply the demand for a hotel of the first-class, suitable for
families, and free from the noise and excitement
incident to the hotels patronized by thousands of
excursionists daily. The building, which stands
1900 feet east of the Manhattan Hotel, is 550 feet
long, and varies in height from three to six
stories. It is built in the Eastern style of architecture, with round towers and lofty minarets,
and presents a remarkably picturesque appearance. It is intended for people who desire the
best accommodations, and who can afford to pay
handsomely therefor, and, as far as possible, it is
intended to exclude excursionists from the house.
There are in all about four hundred sleeping-
rooms in the hotel, which are more elegantly furnished and decorated than those at any other
hotel on the island, and are equal in every respect
to those of the best hotels in the United States.

These are rented at from $3 per day to $10 per day, according to size and location. The restaurant is furnished with the most elegant fixtures and service, and the prices are proportionately higher than at any other hotel. There is no *table d'hôte* at the hotel, and only very slight reductions on the prices of rooms are made even to those who desire to pass the entire season at this house. There is an elevator, gas and running water in every room, and all the luxuries of a first-class city hotel. The house is managed by Messrs. Mackinnie & Co., the proprietors of the Manhattan Hotel.

Oysters are generally supposed from their freshness to be eaten with impunity at the seashore when they are not wholesome at inland places. The rule is well known and pretty generally observed in most cities to abstain from them during the months in the names of which the letter R does not occur ; so that from the beginning of May to the end of August, or the beginning of September, they are not in any great demand, and fortunately at this time clams, crabs and lobsters are at their best. Although, at the seaside, oysters are palatable during the summer season, and are often eaten without apparent harm, there can be no doubt that they sometimes prove treacherous. One is apt occasionally to come across a bad oyster—it may be merely a milky one, or it may be one which is actually spoiled, and the effect of this is to induce a most unpleasant disturbance of the digestive organs. At the best hotels at Coney Island great care is taken in the selection of oysters, but all things considered, they are best left alone at this time of year.

Pedlers.—Comparatively few itinerant vend-ors are now met with on the beach, east of West Brighton. There are a few permitted at Brighton, but they are rigorously excluded from Manhattan Beach. The only class of these vendors who are useful are the men who sell " goggles " or smoked and colored eyeglasses and spectacles. Persons with weak eyes will do well either to provide them-selves beforehand or to purchase from one of these men a pair of colored glasses, as the glare of the sun on the ocean and on the sand at midday is trying to the strongest visual organs. Peanut and popcorn vendors are frequently met with, and en-gage the attention and reap the pennies of children. Scales, where you may try your weight for five cents, will also be met with at points along the shore.

Photographs.—If you should for any reason, personal or otherwise, desire to have your pic-ture taken at Coney Island there is a small pavil-ion devoted to the art near Leach's West End Hotel, and at the Brighton Beach Bathing Pavil-ion. There are generally itinerant photographers also to be met with on the beach. The quality of the pictures taken, of course, rarely surpasses the original, but you don't pay for flattery, but "for the fun of the thing."

Picnics.—Coney Island is essentially a demo-cratic place, where you may do pretty much as you like, and be reasonably sure of not attract-ing any unpleasant amount of notice. You may, if you please, go to Coney Island and spend the day, and enjoy yourself hugely, without expend-ing one cent more than is required to pay your fares to and from the beach. Not only is this possible, but thousands of people, notably moth-

ers with small means and large families, actually
do it every day during the season. At almost
every hotel of any size on the beach there are
tables set apart for the use of parties who bring
their own provisions or lunch baskets, and you
may spread your feast and enjoy it at your pleasure. If you desire you can order beer, clams,
chowder, or the like to supplement your feast,
but there is no obligation to do so implied by
your use of the tables or pavilions, and you will
experience neither rudeness nor neglect. There
are tables for picnic parties at the Manhattan
Pavilion, at the Brighton Beach Bathing Pavilion,
at Bauer's at West Brighton, and at a host of
smaller places there and along the beach to the
West End, where ample accommodations of the
kind will be found in the western part of Norton
& Murray's Pavilion. The places so set apart
are always designated by large signs, so that
you need never fear a rebuff.

Piers.—There are four piers at Coney Island,
only one of which—the New Iron Pier—however,
possesses any interest for the visitor. They are
called Norton's Dock, the West End Pier, Engeman's Pier, and the New Iron Pier (*see* under respective headings).

Planets.—*See* article on SUMMER STARS, *in Appendix.*

Plaza.—The Spanish designation of an open
square (frequently used but not yet incorporated
in the English language by lexicographers), is
the name given to the space at West Brighton
Beach surrounded by hotels and other buildings. It is laid out in grass plots and flower beds,
and intersected by many broad plank walks.
Fountains of drinking water, a great mechanical

Cow, the Observatory, Camera Obscura, and other small structures are scattered about the place.

The mechanical Cow is an enormous bovine which, manipulated by busy dairy maids, dispenses unlimited quantities of ice-cold milk to thirsty visitors at five cents per glass.

Point Breeze—[Map T4]—is at the eastern ex extremity of Coney Island, is the property of the Manhattan Beach Improvement Company, and has Sheepshead Bay on the north and the ocean on the south. It is the eastern terminus of the Marine Railway, and is resorted to by lovers of clam bakes, fish dinners, and rowing and sailing. The view of the ocean, Rockaway Beach, and other points is particularly fine from this place.

Point Breeze Pavilion—[Map, T4]—is at the eastern terminus of the Marine Railway, and is devoted to fish dinners and clam bakes. There are about fifty rooms in the house rented at $1.50 and $2 per day, chiefly to gentlemen sportsmen. At five o'clock every day a Rhode Island clam bake (*see* CLAM BAKES) is served at seventy-five cents per head. Capital fish-dinners may also be ordered here, and row boats and sail boats hired, the former at twenty-five cents and the latter at $1 per hour, or if wanted for a longer time prices by special arrangement. The fishing grounds are near here. (*See* FISHING.)

Point Comfort House — [Map, C4]—between Norton & Murray's and Rosedale, at the west end. It is a small two-story frame building, and has a few bath houses, attached which are labelled "West End Baths." It is one of the many hotels of the cheaper grade at this end of the Island.

Police.—The police force employed on the Island is large enough to preserve perfect order at

all times, and their headquarters are in the AQUA-
RIUM building at West Brighton. The policemen
are mainly paid by the hotel-keepers, but they are
all sworn in as officers by the authorities of
Gravesend. Well-known and capable hotel de-
tectives are also employed by the larger hotels.

Post Office.—There are letter and drop letter
boxes at Brighton and Manhattan Beach Hotels.
Collections are made several times daily.

Prospect Park and Coney Island Railroad runs
from the depot at Ninth Avenue and Twentieth
Street, Brooklyn, to Cable's Hotel, at West
Brighton Beach. The depot is accessible from
Fulton Ferry, Brooklyn, *via* Vanderbilt Avenue
horse-cars. This is frequently called Culver's
road. ☞ *See* TIME-TABLE *in Appendix.*

Punch and Judy.—*See* AQUARIUM.

Race-Courses. — *See* CONEY ISLAND JOCKEY
CLUB and ENGEMAN'S RACE-COURSE.

Railroads.—Coney Island is approached by
six railroads from New York and Brooklyn or
connecting with boats for those places at interme-
diate points. The names of these are as follows:
Brooklyn, Bath and Coney Island Railroad.
Brooklyn and Coney Island Horse Railroad.
Brooklyn, Flatbush and Coney Island Rail·
road.
New York and Manhattan Beach Railroad.·
New York and Sea Beach Railroad.
Prospect Park and Coney Island Railroad.
A description of each of these roads will be
found under separate heads.

Ravenhall—[Map, F4]—is a small neat hostelry
about half of a mile east of the West End Pier. It
contains about a dozen rooms, and bar and res-

taurant. It is resorted to by many men who consider its clam roasts superior to those served at any other place on the Island, albeit the service is a trifle rough.

Restaurants.—Every building on the island, with few exceptions, contains a restaurant, and therefore the choice of a place at which to lunch or dine is one of the greatest perplexities encountered by the stranger or the habitue. The remarks under HOTELS apply equally to restaurants. There is by no means as great a difference in the prices between the higher and lower classes of restaurants as there is in the character of the service and cooking. At the Manhattan, Brighton, and Oriental Hotels, the service and the cooking is on a par with that of the best restaurants in New York, while at the cheaper houses the service is apt to be rough and the cooking indifferent, while the prices are really only a trifle lower than at the better class of restaurants. A nearly uniform tariff has been adopted by common consent for clams cooked in various ways, at the best hotels as well as at the open sheds along the beach, but other viands differ greatly in price, and apparently without any reason or consistency in the gradation. A careful comparison of the prices on the bills of fare, at eight of the representative hotels of their classes on the island, viz. : the Manhattan, Brighton, Bauer's, Engeman's, Vanderveer's, Cable's, Sea Beach, and Iron Pier, gives the following results: Soups are from 20 cents to 25 cents a portion at the cheapest, and from 25 cents to 40 cents at the dearest, an ordinary soup costing about the same at either place. Fish ranges from 35 cents to 50 cents a portion at the cheapest, and from 40 cents to 60 cents at the most expensive, the average price being about the same.

Among roast meats, taking beef as a staple, a portion costs 40 cents at the cheapest, and 50 cents at the dearest, so that as the prices of all the other viands range at about the same comparative rates, it will be seen that in point of price there is but little to choose, and especially is this the case if you exercise care in ordering your dinner. Remember that at all first-class restaurants, where you order more than one course, one portion is ample for two persons. Clams are sold at 20 or 25 cents for raw clams, 40 cents for roast clams, and 25 cents for chowder at all the restaurants on the beach. *See also* DINNERS; FEES; FISH DINNERS.

Rhode Island Clambake.—*See* CLAMBAKES.

Rooms.—*See* HOTELS.

Rosedale—[Map, C–D4]—is a small two-story frame house, which is a resort of the plainer class, and stands about 300 yards west of the West End Pier. It has a small pavilion for picnic parties attached.

Rowing.—Row-boats may be hired at the Pavilion at Point Breeze (which see), accessible *viâ* Marine Railway, fare five cents. The usual price is from twenty-five cents to fifty cents an hour, depending upon the size of the boat, and whether an attendant is required or not. Special rates may be made if you desire to keep the boat many hours. This is the only place on the Island where boating is possible. (*See also* SAILING.)

Sailing.—Good sail-boats may be hired with a competent crew for $1 per hour, or at a less rate if you keep the boat many hours, at Point Breeze (which see), accessible *viâ* Marine Railway fare five cents. This is the only place on the Island where boating is possible. (*See also* ROWING.)

St. Nicholas Hotel — [Map, H4]—is a small house near the landing of the iron pier at West Brighton. It has a bar, restaurant, and shooting gallery, is nicely furnished, and is noticeably neat.

Sanitarium. — The Seaside Home for poor children stands in the rear of the Aquarium. It is a worthy charity, instituted for the purpose of giving the weak and sickly children of the tenement-house districts a week on the seashore.

Sea Beach Hotel [Map H3] is at the terminus of the New York and Sea Beach Railroad at West Brighton. It is not properly a hotel, but a depot and restaurant, and is one of the most attractive looking places on the beach. The building was the United States Government building at the Exposition at Philadelphia in 1876, and is high and roomy as well as graceful in its outlines. The interior is partially surrounded by a balcony, from which Carlberg's orchestra give concerts every afternoon and evening. The east end of the hall is used as a restaurant *à la carte*, and at the west end there is a *table-d'hôte* dinner served daily, at $1 per head, without wine. The trains on the railroad land their passengers in the rear of the hotel, and the beach in front is laid out attractively in flower-beds and grass-plots. In a frame building on the east of the hotel will be found billiard-tables, bowling-alleys, and a shooting-gallery. A broad plank walk leads to the shore end of the Iron Pier, almost directly in front of the building.

Sea Beach Railroad.—*See* NEW YORK AND SEA BEACH RAILROAD.

Seaside Costumes. — *See* BATHING-SUITS; CLOTHING; *also* SURF STYLES, *in Appendix*.

Seaside Home (for Children).—*See* SANITARIUM.

Shooting Galleries, for practice with air-guns, are located at various points along the beach west of the Brighton. The range is ordinarily only about twenty five or thirty feet long, and the tariff for three shots five or ten cents.

Sleight's [Map H4] is a pavilion and restaurant, at popular prices, just east of the landing of the Iron Pier at West Brighton.

Smith's (Mrs.)—[Map, E4]—is a cottage adjoining the Windsor on the east. It contains 10 or 15 rooms, rented at from $5 to $7 each per week, without board.

Soda-Water—at the drug-stores (which *see*).

Spectacles.—*See* PEDDLERS.

Star Gazing.—*See* article on SUMMER STARS, *in Appendix.*

Steam-Orchestrion.—*See* AQUARIUM.

Steamboats.—A number of different steamers from piers on the East and North Rivers run to the Coney Island Pier direct, to Norton's Point direct, and to Locust Grove and Bay Ridge, connecting with railroads at those points for the Beach. To the stranger, the trip *via* the Bay Ridge branch of the New York and Manhattan Beach Road offers great attractions, as it enables him both to see the Bay of New York, and to ride over the most attractive part of the railroad.

☞ *For Time-Tables of all the Steamers, see Appendix.*

Sunday Services are held on Sunday mornings at 11 o'clock in the parlors of the Manhattan Beach Hotel, with music under the direction of Gilmore.

Surf Fashions.—*See* SURF STYLES, *in Appendix.*

Surf House—[Map, G4]—Tilyou's, is a short

distance west of the Iron Pier. The house is neat
and clean, and is, as in former years, the best
family bathing place on the Island. It is still a
quiet, comfortable place, though lacking somewhat
in the conveniences now obtainable elsewhere.
A more than ordinarily good chowder is served
here at 25 cents, and is given gratis to all who
bathe here and pay 25 cents. The price of baths
without the chowder is 20 cents.

Swimming.—*See* article on SWIMMING, *in Appendix.*

Table-d'hôte Dinners.—At the Brighton Beach
Hotel a dinner in five courses, and including
a pint of table claret, is served daily at $1.50
per head, and is extremely well cooked and
served. At the Sea Beach Hotel a *table-d'hôte*
dinner is served without wine at $1 per head,
and on the Iron Pier an excellent dinner in five
courses, including a pint of table claret, is served
at $1 per head. By purchasing dinner tickets at
the shore end of the pier, the price of admission
to the pier (ten cents), is included in this sum.

For persons unaccustomed to ordering their
meals from a bill of fare, this is not only the best,
but the cheapest way to dine.

Telegraph Offices.—These will be found in the
Manhattan, Brighton, Oriental, Cable's, and Nor-
ton & Murray's hotels. Rate for ten words to
New York, twenty-five cents.

Temperature.—The temperature of Coney
Island, as compared with that of New York City,
is of course affected at times by local conditions,
direction of winds, etc., but it is safe to say that it
will average throughout the season ten degrees
lower than the temperature prevailing in New
York.

Tide.—*See* HIGH WATER.

Theatre.—*See* FELTMAN'S.

Tilyou's.—*See* SURF HOUSE.

Tom Thumb.—*See* AQUARIUM.

Trip (The) to Coney Island by Steamer affords the tourist a better idea of the Harbor of New York than he can obtain in any other way. Starting from the pier at the foot of 24th Street, on the North or Hudson River, on the right is Hoboken and the Stevens Castle surmounting the bluff. Then Jersey City on the right, and New York on the left are passed, and the steamer swings round the Battery and Castle Garden. Governor's Island, the headquarters of the Military Department of the East, with its defences, Fort Columbus and Castle William, comes in view on the right as the steamer passes through Buttermilk Channel, which separates it from the Brooklyn shore, which is then on the left, and affords a good view of the Atlantic Docks, which have a pier line 3000 feet long, and a hasin covering forty acres, surrounded by splendid brick and granite warehouses. Staten Island then comes up on the right and the Quarantine Station, and on the left, the Bay Ridge Dock, where there is a depot of the N. Y. and Manhattan Beach Railway. Thence down through the Narrows with the gray walls of Fort Hamilton on the left side, and Fort Wadsworth (formerly Fort Richmond) on the right, and above the latter the green walls of the earthworks called Fort Tompkins. In under the empty port-holes of the ruins of Fort Lafayette, and you pass out into the lower bay. Over to the right lies the low line of Sandy Hook, and nearer the Illinois, a dismantled hulk, and the yellow fever and small-pox floating hospitals,

and Ellis and Bedloe's Islands.   Then Coney
Island comes in view on the left, gay with bunt-
ing, a city of airy castles and a capital of pleasure,
with a new population every day.

Undertow.—*See* article on SWIMMING, *in Appendix.*

Valuables, Care of.—*See* Bathing localities referred to under BATHING.

Vanderveer's Hotel.—*See* OCEAN CONCOURSE
HOTEL.

Van Sicklen's [Map, I1] is a station on the
Prospect Park and Coney Island Railroad at
Coney Island Creek.   It is mainly a resort for
the disciples of Izaak Walton.   (*See* FISHING.)

Waiters' Fees.—*See* FEES.

Ward's —[Map, H4]—is a small hostelry just
west of Feltman's at West Brighton.   It is clean,
neat, and cheap.

West Brighton is the name of that portion of
Coney Island east of the West End and west of
Brighton Beach.   It was formerly known as Culver's Beach.   It is a popular place, and has a
broad plaza in the centre, thickly surrounded by
hotels of various grades, and is the landing-place
of the Iron Pier.

West Brighton Beach Hotel—[Map, H4]
is just east of the landing of the Iron Pier and
fronts on the plaza.   It is kept by Paul Bauer, and
is frequently called Bauer's Hotel.   The building
contains some seventy sleeping rooms, nicely fitted
up, which are rented at $2 to $4 per day and $12 to
$24 per week.   Extending back from the hotel is
a very large pavilion with a wide veranda, in which
are seating and table accommodations for nearly two thousand people.   This contains also a

restaurant, refreshment, and cigar stands, and bar ; and music is furnished by Conterno's Twenty-third Regiment Band, comprising forty pieces. A platform 350 feet long extends out over the ocean, and here you may dine *al ·fresco* with the surf rolling up under your very feet. In the rear a large croquet ground is nicely graded and sodded for the amusement of guests. The hotel is a popular resort, especially for Germans ; and the restaurant is very good. (*See also* PLAZA ; and RESTAURANTS.)

West End Pier—[Map, D4-5]—is an unpainted ramshackle wooden structure, about 450 feet long, projecting into the ocean from a point about three quarters of a mile east of Norton's Point. The Grand Republic, of White's line of steamers, from New York, lands its passengers here. Rosedale Cottage, Half-Way House, and other minor hotels, little better than shanties, are in the vicinity of the pier, and there is a lunch pavilion attached to it.

Windsor—[Map, D4]—is a neat frame cottage at the west end just east of the West End Pier. There is a station on the Prospect Park and Coney Island branch road directly in the rear of this house. The house contains about 25 rooms, which are rented at from $5 to $7 a week each, without board.

APPENDIX.

CONTENTS.

	PAGE
HINTS ON BATHING,	77
SURF STYLES,	83
SWIMMING,	85
THE SUMMER STARS,	95
TIME-TABLES,	111
CALENDAR,	115

HINTS ON BATHING.*

See also BATHING, BATHING SUITS, etc., *in the regular Alphabet.*

*When **not** to Bathe.*—Just after a meal ; or when overfatigued, chilly, or overheated ; or (unless with the sanction of your physician) when suffering from any acute disease or laboring under any organic affection ; or at night, or early in the morning ; or at unseasonable days.

When to Bathe.—When in healthful condition ; when comfortably warm ; two to four hours after

---

* Compiled chiefly from the following excellent little handbooks : Dr. John H. Packard's "Sea Air and Sea Bathing," one of Dr. Keen's admirable Health Primers (Phila., Presley Blakiston) ; Dr. Ghislani Durant's "Sea Bathing : its Use and Abuse" (N. Y., A. Cogswell) ; and Dr. C. Parson's "Sea Air and Sea Bathing," an English publication (Phila., Presley Blakiston).

With a view of diminishing the loss of life which annually occurs from drowning, the Royal Humane Society of England issues the following important advice to bathers : "Avoid bathing within two hours after a meal, or when exhausted by fatigue or from any other cause, or when the body is cooling after perspiration, and avoid bathing altogether in the open air if, after being a short time in the water, there is a sense of chilliness, with numbness of the hands and feet, but bathe when the body is warm, provided no time is lost in getting into the water. Avoid chilling the body by sitting or standing undressed on the banks or in boats, after having been in the water, or remaining too long in the water, but leave the water immediately there is the slightest feeling of chilliness. The vigorous and strong may bathe early in the morning on an empty stomach, but the young and those who are weak had better bathe two or three hours after a meal ; the best time for such is from two to three hours after breakfast. Those who are subject to attacks of giddiness or faintness, and who suffer from palpitation and other sense of discomfort at the heart, should not bathe without first consulting their medical adviser."

a meal, at any time between 7 A.M. and 7 P.M. (from beginning of June to end of September). Best time immediately before and during HIGH WATER (*which see in the regular Alphabet*).

Before the Bath.—When overheated take, before undressing, a moderate walk until perspiration has subsided ; don't try to cool off in bathing dress ; don't wait until entirely cooled off; slightly warm from moderate exercise rather heightens the bracing effects of the bath.

Entering the Bath.—Enter resolutely and briskly, until the water reaches the waist ; then plunge headlong or allow a wave to break over your head—all sensations of fear, dislike, chilliness or danger of congestion are thus at once dispelled. At any rate, wet immediately both chest and abdomen before you " clutch the rope."

How to Bathe.—Whatever you do, keep moving and duck under. A common practice with people who cannot swim, says Dr. Durant, is to wade out until the water reaches the waist, stand still, and from time to time immerse the remainder of the body as far as the shoulders, *allowing the head to remain dry.* A more injurious method of bathing can scarcely be imagined. If the bather desires a foot-bath, he had better by far obtain it in his own room. For those who have not learned how to swim, the best plan is to walk out quickly into the water (at least breast deep) then by moving about quickly, using both legs and arms, they may obtain satisfactory results. If, however, the bather prefers the surf to smooth water, the best way to proceed is to let the waves strike the *lateral* or the *posterior* portions of the body, allowing himself frequently to be entirely submerged. We would, however, advise all who

propose to bathe in the sea for any length of time
to *learn to swim.* A knowledge of the art not
only gives the bather more confidence in himself,
but allows him to enjoy the water to an extent
that otherwise would be impossible. In this
exercise we find combined all the conditions
necessary to attain, and that in a pleasing manner,
the most beneficial effects of sea-water upon the
system. (*See* article on SWIMMING, *in Appendix*.)

How long and how often to bathe.—Five to fifteen
minutes by the watch (if you have any to consult)
should be the average duration of a bath. A
safer guide is to leave the water as soon as the
second chill is felt. The *first* sense of cold is
felt on entering the water, which is soon followed
by the feeling of returning warmth. The second
cooling, then, shown specially by blueness of the
lips or finger-nails, should *invariably* be the signal
for leaving the water *at once.* There are men " to
the water born," who can live in, if not on, water ;
but every one should consult his own skin. The
same remark applies to the "how often." One
bath a day is enough for most people, although
robust people may occasionally enter twice a day
unharmed, and extraordinary people as often as
they please. Some people don't mind headache,
nausea, biliousness, syncope, etc., some do.

After the bath.—If the day be very warm,
says Dr. Durant, the bather, after quitting the
water, may, sheltering himself from the wind,
remain in his bathing-dress and allow it to dry
upon his person. This we think the best plan,
as it permits the deposits of the saline particles
on the skin, and by their stimulating action in-
sures reaction. Generally, however, walk briskly
to the bathing-house and rub the body dry with
a coarse towel until a healthy glow is produced,

When opportunity offers wash the head, previous to drying the body, with fresh water, so as to free the hair from salt, which would make it stiff and harsh (Packard), or to avoid those troublesome headaches (Durant). Moderate exercise, a short walk (not in the sun) on the beach, or a piazza, are advisable before giving yourself up to the demands of a vigorous appetite or the temptations of the table.

Children ought never to be forced into the surf. —All the good effects which are expected from the bathing, says Dr. Packard, are nullified by the fright and nervous shock. The proper way is to get them gradually accustomed to the sea ; to let them have their bathing-clothes on, and play on the beach, when they will go to the edge of the water, and by-and-by find their own way in. Or they may be very gently tempted in by constant efforts, always seeing that they do not get frightened, or, if they do, letting them have plenty of time to become reassured. If they find that, after all, they are not hurt, and that no attempt is made to force them in, they will soon gain confidence.

Irritation of the Skin.—Not unfrequently a sea-bath is attended by a more or less troublesome irritation of the skin, for which the chemical composition of sea-water is a sufficient explanation. Most bathers will suffer no annoyance from this irritation, but with some persons it amounts to positive discomfort. In referring to this matter, Dr. Parsons observes: "The skin becomes rose-colored, sometimes scarlet, with elevated points scattered over the surface, giving rise occasionally to groundless alarm ; and there is much burning, tingling, and itching, particularly at night or when the body is warmed by exercise.

But these unpleasant symptoms gradually subside as soon as the skin has become accustomed to the bath, and no further inconvenience is experienced."

Headache.—Persons subject to headache are more or less liable to trouble in this direction, either during or after the bath, especially if their entrance into the water gives them too great a shock or if they remain in or under the water too long. "Occasionally," says Dr. Parsons, "congestive headache results from bathing too soon after a full meal or in the heat and glare of the midday sun." If due care is exercised in regard to the time selected for the bath, the unpleasant effect may be avoided, while in the case of persons of nervous temperament, with whom, not unfrequently, "the very anticipation of the bath is sufficient to cause throbbing pain in the head, which immersion in the sea only intensifies, an effectual preventive will be found in the precaution of thoroughly wetting the head and making it perfectly cool before entering the water."

Nausea and Faintness.—A weak stomach sometimes rebels against indulgence in a sea-bath, often accompanying its protests with nausea and vomiting after the bath, or, in the case of delicate women, with faintness also. Persons so inclined should not bathe before breakfast, or after too long abstinence from food, as the system is not sufficiently fortified to withstand the shock of immersion. Says Dr. Parsons on this point: "A glass of wine and rest in the recumbent posture will obviate the distressing symptoms; but common-sense dictates that the bath should never be attempted when the body is exhausted, and the circulation lowered by the want of food."

6

Water in the Ear.—Considerable annoyance is frequently caused by the water getting into the ears of bathers, particularly if they dive below the surface, or if there is a strong surf; and it is affirmed that deafness, requiring medical treatment for its relief, has sometimes followed as a result. By way of precaution against the entrance of the water, says Dr. Packard, it is well to put a small piece of cotton *lightly* in to each ear before going into the sea. . . . The best way of getting rid of the water is that usually resorted to by boys after swimming, viz., to turn the head well over toward the affected side, putting a finger in the opposite ear, and then to hop about on one foot. A few moments of this exercise will generally cause the water to escape in a stream.

SURF STYLES FOR THE SEASON 1880.

From the N. Y. Herald, May 31, 1880.

Bathing-dresses are as fanciful and striking as the taste of the wearer may elect and are no longer considered indelicate if they follow the outline of the form to some little extent. Favor is about equally divided between the blouse costume and the swimming costume, which latter is not so cumbrous in the water as the former. A novelty in bathing-shoes consists of a canvas sandal laced across the instep and quite high at the back; the sole is of perforated brass, with small straps of leather under toe and heel. A fine brass network covers the perforations and prevents the sand from penetrating inside. There is a thin cork sole next the brass and over this a thin leather one, all perforated to let out the water. Almost all ladies object to bathing on the score of clumsy suits. With a pair of these bathing-shoes over the stockings the drawers need only reach the knees, the blouse need not be so long and the sleeves had either better be omitted, made very short or cut to fit the arm closely as the fashionable dress sleeve. The waist should be cut very high on the shoulders, so that the arm-hole clears the joint of the shoulder, and there will be no excuse for sore arms in the effort of swimming. If the arms and neck burn easily have the bathing costume made low in the neck, with only a strip across the shoulder, like the fashionable ball dress, and wear a scarlet or blue gauze vest, with high neck and long sleeves. A mixed nautical cotton and wool is best adapted to bathing, as it does not shrink like all wool, and does not heft with the water like all cotton.

Among the new fabrics shown for seaside costumes is zephyr cloth, a fine cotton material with a woollen finish ; tally-ho suitings, all wool, in old gold ; Havana and French gray, all made up, either all of one shade or with admixtures of other colors and fabrics. Black silk is highly favored by the frequenters of the camp-meetings, the " L " and " T " brand of family silk being highly commended for elegance of finish, lustre and wearing qualities. American silks bid fair to rival the finest importations, some of those now in the market being considered unsurpassed in all the qualities that commend a good silk to favorable notice. For cool days out-of-town the American black silk and satin de Lyon are considered almost indispensable to every well-dressed lady's wardrobe.

SWIMMING.

"Leander" in the Illustrated Christian Weekly.

As swimming is a healthy exercise and pleasant amusement, and as proficiency gives the expert the power to save his own life as well as the lives of others, the acquirement of the art should be encouraged by parents, teachers, and also by the authorities. In France it is considered a necessary part of the boy's education, and the regular soldier is trained to swim, not only that he may save himself and comrades, but be more useful in building bridges, and all other work in the water incidental to military life.

Females can and do learn to swim as easily as males, and their physical education should not be called complete until they have been taught to swim, because the expert male swimmer is often drowned in the attempt to save the female when she does not know how to support herself in the water, and cripples him by her frantic efforts to cling to him. Happily this has been considered of late years in New York, and the free swimming-baths for both sexes have not only educated a generation of experts among that class who are most exposed to the perils of the water, but have been the means of conserving the public health in a marked degree. Every day in the papers we see accounts of persons being saved from drowning. To-day the newsboy or bootblack of a dozen summers, waiting his turn to get into the free bath, saves a comrade who has fallen off the dock ; to-morrow the uniformed policeman risks his own life to save the would-be suicide or the helpless inebriate. Upon inquiry you will nearly always find he is a graduate of the New York docks or the free-swimming-baths.

There are several methods of swimming : the most common is forward, face downward, being illustrated by the accompanying cut. The theory of swimming depends upon the simple principle that if a force is applied to any body, it will move in the direction where there is the least resistance. This is seen in the motion of vessels and takes place in swimming, whether the animal be man, quadruped, bird, or fish. Directions to acquire the art have been elaborated until the person who cannot swim is appalled by their number, and concludes it must be a very difficult thing to do, and therefore dreads the water and never tries to learn.

Caution! Do not undress and dash into the water after a long walk or run, or when much heated. Do not enter the water when the stomach is entirely empty, nor when you are fatigued by either hard mental or physical labor. The most common cause of cramp in the legs or arms is due to ignorance of or neglect of these simple precautions. Do not go into the water sooner than two or three hours after a hearty meal, as it interferes with digestion and nullifies any good to be obtained by the exercise. For beginners especially : Do not stay in the water too long ; ten minutes, or at most twenty, will be enough for one not accustomed to the water.

Walk gently into the water breast-deep, wet the head and neck with the hands, lie down lightly, face downward, holding head and neck well up, keeping the eyes fixed upward. Strike out with both feet from the bottom, at the same time shoving the hands forward, palm-to-palm to the full length of the arms, sweep the arms around not quite a quarter circle (as seen in illustration),

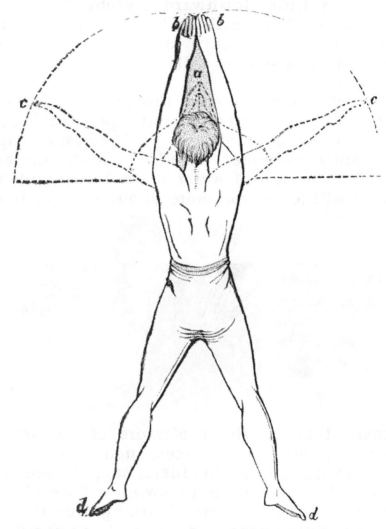

turning the palm of the hand gradually outward to get the largest pulling power against the water. The arms are drawn back quickly, elbows close to the ribs, hands together as before, feet drawn up as close to the body as possible, and the motions repeated as before. The stroke of the feet should be in time with the pulling sweep of the hands, to get the most speed with the least waste of strength. The stroke of the feet should be also a little downward thereby lifting the breast upward and making the breathing easier. Don't try to do too much at one lesson ! If you can swim three strokes without going under, it is a fair start.

A great many become discouraged and say, " Oh, I can't learn to strike out right, I can't keep time with my legs and arms." The best example of a natural swimmer is the frog. Catch one and put him in a tub of water or an aquarium-tank, and he will teach you more about the way to do

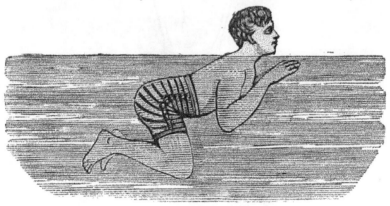

it easily than all the professors of swimming. There are many appliances, such as life-belts, cork-jackets, inflated bladders, etc., recommended as aids in learning to swim. They should not be used, as the person learning even the motions perfectly by their use is nearly always timid without them. Diving, floating, swimming on the back, on the side, etc., are all easily learned after the pupil has acquired the method described above.

A recent English writer well says : " Man is the only animal that drowns unnecessarily. He does so because the knowledge he ought to possess

does not come to his rescue, as does the instinct
of the brute. A dog, or a horse, or any other
quadruped, when it finds itself out of its depth,
swims away with its head above water, and
usully gets safe to land. Man not finding himself in his natural position, is filled with terror,
stretches his hands out of the water, which helps
him to sink, or opens his mouth to scream, which
fills his lungs with water instead of air. The result is obvious. If we could only have faith in
the natural buoyancy of the body, and when cast
unexpectedly upon the water, remain passively
upon it, *with the mouth tightly closed*, many lives
might be saved that are now annually lost."

Sanford B. Hunt in St. Nicholas.

In a practical and most instructive article in
St. Nicholas (volume for 1877) entitled "A Talk
about Swimming," Mr. Sanford B. Hunt makes
the following hints and suggestions : " Get accustomed to the shock of water. Wade slowly out,
then turn and face the shore ; duck under in
water deep enough to cover the body (say two
feet), get your head wet, hold your breath when
under, snort as you come to the air again, resist-
ing the inclination to breathe in first ; and then
in a depth of a foot or two lie down, face downward, and touch the tips of your fingers on the
sand or the bed of the stream. You will find
that a very slight lift, hardly two ounces, will
keep your head afloat, but not your heels. Use
them as oars. Drop out backward into deeper
water, walking on your finger tips, and you will
find that the more of your body there is under
the water the less weight you have to carry. The
only parts to keep in the air are your lips and

nostrils. Make these the only exposed surface; hollow your loins and carry your head well back, so as to have it perpendicular to the lungs. All this is mere paddling ; but you will soon find that keeping afloat is no trouble, unless you keep too high and try to swim as much in the air as in the water. In swimming you must lie low. The legs should be well under and so should the hands ; the chin in the water, the legs at an angle of thirty-three degrees. The theory is that you should use the feet as a counterpoise to the head —the chest, the buoyant part of the body, being the fulcrum of the lever. If your heels go up, your head will go down. Now stop paddling, abandon the grip of your hands on the bottom, keep your head toward the shore and strike out. Two feet depth of water is enough for the lesson.

"Keep both hands well under water. You can't swim in the air. Hold your fingers together, the palms of the hands slightly hollowed, the head well back, the chest inflated, and strike with all four limbs in unison of movement. The hands and the feet will act as propellers, the hands moving backward and downward as low as the hips and well outside of the body, the feet draw-ing together and pushing down at the same mo-ment. Give full spread to your hands and feet. Their resistance to the water is your propelling force. Then gather, frog fashion, and repeat the motion. You rid yourself of the sense of danger by keeping in shallow water and striking toward shore. Work in that way a while and the tempta-tions will be irresistible to swim *from* shore ; but this temptation should be very carefully indulged until you feel sure of yourself."

Floating.—With regard to floating, Mr. Hunt remarks : "It needs only self-possession and

still water. One attitude which seems the most
scientific, but which I never worked with any
considerable success, is to lie upon your back
with only the mouth and nostrils out of water,
and the arms, extended backward, balancing the
legs, the lungs being at the fulcrum of the lever.
I have seen such floating done without the motion of a muscle, except that the lungs were kept
inflated. But as a personal habit I float better
with my legs deeper in the water, and my hands
wrapped under the small of my back, the body
in a semi-perpendicular position. You have
plenty of time to breathe if you are only self-
confident." (*See also* FLOATING, *below.*)

Cautionary.—The following cautions are from
Dr. Packard's " Sea Air and Sea Bathing : "
It is not safe to swim in the sea when the tide
is running out, as then it is difficult to make
headway towards the shore. (*See* HIGH WATER
in regular Alphabet.)

It is not safe to swim when there is a heavy surf,
as even a good swimmer may be so confused and
baffled by waves breaking over him as to lose his
presence of mind and perhaps swim seaward instead of to the shore ; or he may be so exhausted
by the force of the water as to sink.

It is not safe to swim when there are strong
currents in the general line of the shore, as these
sometimes set outward enough to keep the
bather in deep water longer than his powers can
hold out. Should he find himself in such a
current, he should never try to make head
directly against it, but should swim diagonally
towards the shore, and above all, should try to
keep his presence of mind, and save his strength.

Cramp, although much less apt to occur in sea

than in river bathing, is sometimes brought on
if the water is very cold. The person affected
should be at once helped ashore, when warmth
and frictions will probable give speedy relief.
No person subject to this very painful affection
should swim unless a boat is constantly close at
hand.

When a swimmer becomes *exhausted,* if he will
turn on his back and float, he can often regain
his strength, and with it his self-possession. This
latter is of the utmost possible importance ; the
moment it is lost, and the bather begins to
struggle and to call for help, the danger is im-
minent. A *swimmer* should never lose his
courage.

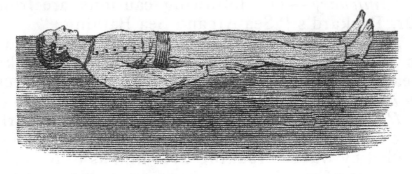

Floating is a very pleasant form of bathing, and
easily learned if one has only confidence. It
consists in turning on the back, and keeping the
nose and mouth out of the water. Of course
this cannot be done when the surf is very rough,
and it is best always to have some one near, lest,
without his knowledge, a current or the tide
should carry the floater out into deep water.
Lives have been lost for want of this precaution.
(*See also* FLOATING *above.*)

Danger of the Piers.—The piers, stretching out
several hundred feet into the ocean, not only

enable one to obtain a different and much finer view of the surf than is possible from the beach, but they also afford the luxury of a breeze even when little or no air is stirring on the beach. Swimmers, however, cannot be too cautious in regard to bathing at these piers. Their effect upon the beach itself, is not good, as they act upon the principle of the jetty, in deepening the water in their vicinity. They are most dangerous as refuges for exhausted swimmers, as I have more than once seen. A man makes out to reach one of them and clings to the supporting piles, with the waves breaking over him continually, since either to climb up on the pier or to sustain himself above the level of the wave-crests is no easy matter after a long swim for life ; hence, unless assistance comes in some other way, he must soon be washed off.

Undertow.—To a greater or less extent the undertow—" that merciless drag backward of the sea, the topmost wave washing the swimmer illusively toward the shore, the undermost sucking him down and out "—exists at all our Northern beaches. As a matter of course all the water that rolls shoreward in a heavy surf must go back again. On this point, Mr. Hunt, in his *St. Nicholas'* article, remarks : " The top-sea rolls in and the under-sea rolls out. Trust to the former. Keep clear afloat, and as high as you can. Secure the friendship of the shoreward wave. Otherwise, if, when you are within ten feet of shore and safety, you drop your legs to the angle of thirty-three degrees, which is the deepest swimming position, you will find that the undertow will grab you by the ankles and pull you out and down again. Keep clear afloat ; your head well down, your heels feeling the topmost of the impelling wave. Keep your lungs well filled **and** wash ashore. You are not safe until **you can** easily fasten your hands in the sand or gravel, and pull yourself to land. But in shallow water, with a long surf rolling in behind you, **the drag** of the undertow can only be avoided by swimming high and letting the waves ' buck ' you in. *Swim shallow and trust the topmost wave.*"

Safety-hint.—A person in danger close to the shore, may often be reached and drawn in by **a** line of men joining hands. This only needs coolness and courage on the part of the outermost men of the line (who should be the tallest) and above all, firmness of grip."

" One never can be alone if he is familiarly acquainted with the stars. He rises early in the summer morning that he may see his winter friends: in winter, that he may gladden himself with a sight of summer stars. He hails their successive rising as he does the coming of his personal friends from beyond the sea."—HENRY WHITE WARREN.

THE SUMMER STARS.*

The following brief directions have no other object than to introduce a new element of pleasure into the long summer evenings spent at the seaside. No attempt is made at scientific explanation, the most direct mode being chosen for pointing out in the grand picture gallery of the heavens the most beautiful and favorite pictures, such as can be easily found and detached, named and remembered, and such, indeed, as, once recognized, will never be forgotten. Should a few hours thus spent in quiet contemplation kindle in some the desire to know more about the nature of the heavenly bodies, let him take up one of the books (mentioned below) from which we have gathered these crumbs, and he will find himself richly rewarded by the study. One such result in a thousand or ten thousand would indeed make

* Compiled from the following popular hand-books, all of which can be safely recommended for more serious study: Proctor's " Half-Hours with the Stars ;" Proctor's " Half-Hours with the Telescope" (New York: Putnams) ; and James Freeman Clarke's " How to Find the Stars" (Boston : Lockwood, Brooks & Co.). A few popular descriptions have been taken from Newcomb's " Popular Astronomy," the most extensive of the works mentioned, and H. W. Warren's " Recreations in Astronomy" (both, N. Y. : Harpers) ; also from Proctor's entertaining series of articles in the *St. Nicholas*, for 1877, which is to appear in book-form shortly.

amends for the existence of this butterfly guide, which, skimming the surface without a why and wherefore, has no eye but for tangible beauty, or beauty that can be *felt* without telescope.

Any one not already familiar with some of the constellations is cautioned not to attempt too much on the same evening. Let him read up and commit to memory all that is said on one constellation. The finding and study of one or two constellations is quite an encouraging beginning, and their recognition, on subsequent evenings, is only a small foretaste of the pleasure that will increase with increasing acquaintance. Don't be discouraged by the bewildering confusion of the first attempts to detect a certain star picture. Your eyes have to travel many times over the skies before they will learn to recognize at a glance your friends among the millions.

Finding the Pole Star.

(Popularly known as the " North Star.")

First look for *Ursa Major,* the Great Bear. Standing on the beach facing the ocean, turn right about face, look up, toward the left (northwest), and you cannot miss the familiar set of seven bright stars of the Great Bear, better known as the *Dipper,* owing to its shape, four of the stars forming its cup, three its handle.* The two end stars (of the cup, or the most distant from the handle, and at this season the lowest†) are called the *Pointers,* because they always

---

* Suspended from the two lower stars are two tassels, each consisting of three stars, two near each other at the end of the tassel, and the third nearer the Dipper. Another pair of small stars make a third tassel.—CLARKE.

† Supposing you look for the Dipper at various seasons, say at nine o'clock in the evening, you will see it in the various

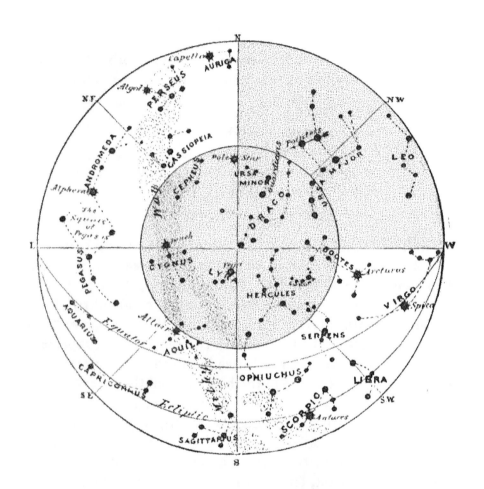

SUMMER STAR MAP.

[*See Explanation on next page.*]

EXPLANATION .OF MAP.

This map is a reproduction of one of Proctor's Star Maps, giving, as follows, the approximate position of the more prominent stars during summer:

End of June—toward midnight.
Middle of July—toward eleven o'clock.
End of July—toward ten o'clock.
Middle of August—toward nine o'clock.
End of August—toward eight o'clock.

The shifting of the stars during the intervening hours can be followed by bearing in mind that stars seen at a certain hour and place will appear on the same spot three to four minutes sooner on the following evening, or about two hours earlier a month later. (*See also*, p. 100, "The Apparent Motion of the Stars.") In this map the central point represents the point over the observer's head, and the circumference his horizon. Thus, if at one of the hours named the observer wishes to find "Aquila," its position on the map shows where to look for it toward the S. E. (southeast), about midway between zenith and horizon. Next, if at one of the hours named the observer wishes to learn what stars are visible toward the west and southwest, let him turn the map until the portion of the circumference between W. and S. W. is *lowermost*, and he will see that in the direction named lies "Bootes" in prominent position.

Some allowance should be made, in the star map, for a small difference of the horizon, chiefly noticeable north and south. Thus, while in the south Scorpio and Sagittarius are seen higher above the horizon at the hours indicated, "Auriga," at the extreme north, will rise into full view later in the season.

point to the *Pole Star*. This star is easily found by drawing a line through the Pointers (from the star in the bottom of the cup to the end star) and following this direction a short distance*—the first bright star you meet is the Pole Star.

The Pole Star.—This found, you have a known central point, and your never-failing compass, for wherever you may stand, facing the Pole Star, the north lies before you, the south behind you, the east on your right, the west on your left. The Pole Star lies always in the same position, or so nearly so that if, for example, you have once been shown or found out that from a certain spot in your garden, or from a certain window in your house, it can be seen just above a certain chimney or tree, you will find it in this direction on any starry night, at any time of the year.

The Pole Star belongs to the constellation of *Ursa Minor* or the Smaller Bear, and figures in its tail ; or, if you prefer the more popular picture, in the handle of the *Little Dipper*. Both Dippers are of similar shape, except that the handles bend in, and always point to, opposite directions, and that, some of the stars of the Little Dipper are much fainter. The two end stars, which with the Pole Star are the brightest of the constellation, and which correspond with the Pointers in the Dipper, viz., being the end stars of the cup, are called the *Guardians of the Pole*,

---

positions as follows : Above the Pole Star (north of the zenith) in April and May ; west of the Pole Star (west of north), the Pointers downward (lowest) ; close to the north horizon, in October and November; east of the Pole Star, the Pointers highest, in January and February.

* It will be of much help to get some idea of distance in degrees. The two stars of the Pointers are 5 degrees apart ; thus following the Pointers nearly five times this distance (29 degrees) we come to the Pole Star.

"because they circle around it," according to Proctor, " as though keeping watch and ward over the axle-end of the great star-dome."

The Apparent Motion of the Stars.*—Stand facing the Pole Star. Then all the stars are travelling round that star in *a direction contrary to that in which the hands of a watch move.* Thus the stars below the pole are moving *toward the right,* those above the pole *toward the left,* those to the right of the pole *upward* (from the east), those to the left of the pole downward (to the west).

Next face the south. Then all the stars on our left, that is, toward the east, are rising slantingly toward the south; those due south are moving horizontally to the right, that is, toward the west, and those on our right are passing slantingly downward toward the west.†

The annual motion of the stars takes place in exactly the same manner as the daily motion.‡

---

*The seeming motions of the sun and the stars, as they travel from east to west, or seem to rise in the east and set in the west, are *not real* movements of their own, but made to appear as such by the actual movement or spinning of the earth from west to east. There *are* real or proper motions of the stars, but not perceptible to the naked eye. The chief and most wonderful peculiarity of the fixed stars, says Clarke, is that they virtually never change their positions in relation to each other. Thus the forms of constellations appear unaltered for thousands of years.

† In a clear night the heavens seem like a vast dome studded with stars. They appear to rise in the east and sweep, like a mighty army, perfectly disciplined, west. If each left its line of march marked by a tracery of golden fire, we should have a dome of parallel lines in perfect circles. And if we should go south of the equator new stars would appear circling in another dome, and all concentric at the south pole. All these stars seem to be at the same distance.—HENRY W. WARREN.

‡ " By the revolution of the earth, which turns on its axis every twenty-four hours, every observer is brought round once a day to every point of the heavens, except that portion which

If we view the sky at ten o'clock on any night, and again, at the same hour one month later, we shall find that at the latter observation the heavens appear to have rotated by the *twelfth* part of a complete circumference, and the appearance presented is precisely the same we should have observed had we waited for two hours (the *twelfth part* of a day) on the day of the first observation.— (PROCTOR.)

South, Southeast, and East.

Face the Ocean : it is toward the south that the heavens present the most glorious display during summer.

Scorpio, the chief summer constellation (resembling a scorpion with extended claws), is in full view above the horizon in June and July ; descending southwest in August. The bright, ruddy star is *Antares* (the Heart of the Scorpion), a star of first magnitude, and perhaps the most beautiful of all the red stars. The word "Antares" means, in fact, "the rival of Mars." It has a smaller star on each side and a long curved row of stars to the west.

Antares sets during August between 12 and 10 ; September, 10 and 8 P.M.

Sagittarius, the Archer, is fully above the horizon in July, closely following Scorpio. It comprises a large collection of second magnitude stars east of Scorpio and in and east of the

---

is hidden by the rotundity of the earth itself. To an observer in the Northern Hemisphere all parts of the heavens become visible every year, except the region around the Southern Pole. Were it not for the daylight, which eclipses a portion, we should see all the other stars once in every twenty-four hours. But during the year we have an opportunity, by the revolution of the earth in its orbit, to see them all except those at the extreme south."—JAMES FREEMAN CLARKE.

Milky Way. Its chief stars resemble a bow and arrow, the arrow directed toward the scorpion.

Saggitarius is followed from the east by *Capricornus,* the She-Goat, and this, in same direction, by *Aquarius,* the Water-bearer, neither of which have any remarkable stars. These (*all* along the horizon) are followed by *Pegasus* (which *see* further on.)

*The Milky Way, or Galaxy,** in a clear, starlight night, at this season, makes a fine display, spanning the skies from north to south. Its superior brilliancy toward the south indicates its greater proximity in that direction.

As some of the most prominent constellations lie along or near the Milky Way, we will, starting from Sagittarius, point out these first, by following the cloudy stream from south to north ; but the Milky Way being only in good sight on clear dark nights, we will also indicate their position independent of this path.

Aquila, the Eagle.—Following upward the larger branch of the Milky Way, or looking above Sagittarius, eastward, about midway between zenith and horizon, we strike three bright stars in cross-way line (six degrees long), which form the

---

* To the naked eye so much of the Galaxy as can be seen at one time presents the appearance of a white, cloud-like arch resting on two opposite points of the horizon, and rising to a greater or less altitude, according to the position of the celestial sphere relative to the observer. Only one half of the entire arch can be seen above the horizon at once, the other half being below it and directly opposite the visible half. Indeed, there is a portion of it which can never be seen at our latitude, being so near the south pole that it is always below the horizon. If the earth were removed, or made transparent, so that we could see the whole celestial sphere at once, the Galaxy would appear as a complete belt extending around it. The telescope shows that the Galaxy arises from the light of countless stars (estimated over ·18,000,000), too minute to be separately visible with the naked eye.—SIMON NEWCOMB.

head of the Eagle. The finely scintillating star in the middle, called *Altair*, is of first magnitude, the other two are of third magnitude. Five or six other stars extending and spreading below Altair give the shape of the constellation. Parts of the Milky Way, near and in the Eagle, are very bright, and even with a small telescope seem to be crowded with stars.

Altair reaches south, in August, between 11 and 9 ; middle of September, 8 P.M.

Cygnus, the Swan.—Beyond the Eagle, further up, and directly in the Milky Way, you will notice six stars forming a conspicuous cross (or as Proctor remembered it in his boyhood, "a capital kite"), twenty degrees long by seventeen degrees wide, its chief star, *Deneb*, heading it. The cross is east, in a horizontal position, nearer zenith than midway in July ; in Aug. and Sept. approaching the zenith, the upright and cross-rod of the cross equally inclined to the horizon. Near Deneb there is seen a straight dark rift, and near this space is another larger cavity, which has been termed the northern *Coal-sack*. The western branch of the Milky Way is covered by a large oval mass exceedingly rich and brilliant.

Lyra, the Harp. — Near the zenith, west and southwest of the Swan, and above, north and northwest of the Eagle, shines the bright *Vega*, the principal star of Lyra,* of first magnitude and of a brilliant white color with a tinge of blue.

---

* The Harp, the Swan and the Eagle can be struck at once by looking up, east (later more south-southwest), between midway and zenith—the three brightest stars standing out against all the others, form an immense and very striking (isoscles) triangle. They are : the lowest, Altair of the Eagle; the highest, Vega of the Harp ; and north or east of these Deneb of the Swan, all stars of the first magnitude.

This and two faint stars (two degrees only from each other) form a beautiful little triangle, nearly equilateral.

Pegasus, the Winged-Horse.—Below, east of Deneb in the Swan (top of cross), Pegasus is rising into view, easily recognized by four stars of second magnitude, which form the large *Square of Pegasus,* three stars belonging to Pegasus, and the fourth (northeast corner) to Andromeda, which follow later in the season, Pegasus from the northeastern horizon.

The Square is above the horizon toward end of June at 11, end of July at 9 P.M.

The Dolphin and Sagitta.—Although but very small constellations, formed by rather faint stars, their symmetrical forms make them easily discernible. The *Dolphin,* sometimes called "Job's Coffin," four or five stars in diamond shape, is between the Square of Pegasus and Altair of the Eagle. *Sagitta,* or the Arrow, is the smallest constellation, formed by four stars, of fourth magnitude, to be found, near the Dolphin, above the Eagle and below the Swan.

South, Southwest, West.

Bootes, the Bearkeeper.—Look for the Dipper (see directions above). Continuing the curve of the handle (about the same distance as is between the Pointers and the Pole Star, viz., about thirty degrees), you strike the most brilliant star in the southwestern skies. This is *Arcturus,* the "ruddy star" of Bootes, a fine constellation which, in the western skies, retains a prominent position during the whole summer. Arcturus, on account of its brilliancy, is seen early in the evening. Above Arcturus the constellation is reaching high up, presenting "a fine figure as with uplifted arm (formed by the stars of the Crown, which *see below*) he chases the Great Bear round the zenith." The smaller brilliant star (orange and green, above Arcturus and nearly central of the constellation) is known as *Mirac*, also on account of its extreme beauty (through the telescope) called "Pulcherrima" (the most beautiful). The curve of the handle of the Dipper continued through Arcturus further down, west (about forty degrees), strikes Spica of *Virgo* (the Virgin), another star of first magnitude and visible until of August.

Arcturus sets in September between 10.30 and 8.30 P.M.

Virgo, the Virgin, is not far above the western horizon ; somewhat in the shape of a big rounded Y in horizontal position, formed by Spica as base and the curve of the stars above it. Virgo is closely following, from the southwest to west, downward, *Leo*, the Lion, which is approaching the horizon, in the shape of a sickle inclined forward, the bright star, *Regulus*, in the handle.

Spica sets in August, Regulus in July, between 10 and 8 P.M.

Fomalhaut.—Later in the season, the bright star of Fomalhaut, belonging to the small constellation *Pisces Austrealis*, the Southern Fish, will make its solitary appearance low in the southern region.

Ophiuchus, the Serpent-bearer and the *Serpent.* —Below, or south of Bootes, above, or north of Scorpio and west of the Milky Way we find this pair of constellations. Ophiuchus stands with one foot on Scorpio, while his head is marked high up by a star of the second magnitude, the figure occupying one third to one fourth of the way from the zenith to the horizon. The Serpent, which he holds in his hands, lies with its tail in an opening of the Milky Way, southwest of the Eagle, while its neck and head are formed by a collection of small stars some distance north of Scorpio, and extending up to the borders of Bootes. It is very difficult for the beginner to get clear boundaries of these combined constellations. He may notice a fine line of six bright little stars, inclined toward west; the lower three, south, belong to Ophiuchus, the upper three to the Serpent. These stars, with the brightest star at the eastern end of the line, and a curve of two smaller stars at the western end, resemble somewhat the form of a monstrous sword or curved sabre, the cross handle being formed by two stars, one above and one below the line.*

Hercules.—High up, east of Bootes, west of Lyra, and north of Ophiuchus, Hercules extends up toward the zenith. It contains no striking star, but is easily recognized by its containing a rather irregular quadrangle. A straight line drawn from the fifth and third star of the Dipper (counting from the handle) will strike it.

Draco, the Dragon, lies with his head just north of Hercules, the head represented by three stars in an equilateral triangle; the body, seven faint stars, forms a long curved line bending round between the Great and the Little Dipper.

---

* The large constellation Ophiuchus is not specially interesting. The figure is an absurd one, the legs being singularly feeble. But it must be admitted he is awkwardly placed. The serpent is quite enough to occupy his attention, yet a scorpion is ready to sting one leg and to pinch the other. The club of Hercules may be meant for the serpent, and the arrow of the Archer for the scorpion, but they seem to threaten the Serpent-Bearer as much.—PROCTOR *in St. Nicholas*, 1877.

Corona Borealis, the Northern Crown, a smaller constellation east of and close to Bootes, west of Hercules, and just above the Serpent's head, is composed of a pretty semi-circle of six stars, supposed to form a chaplet or crown. The third nearest Bootes, the most brilliant, is *Alpherat*, a star of second magnitude.

North, Northeast.

The northern region, in strange contrast to the brilliant southern sky, shows no large stars and no prominent constellation is in good position for observation with the exception of *Cassiopeia*, or the Lady in the Chair, readily recognized by five stars (northeast, in the Milky Way), in the form of an open "straggling" W. It is on the opposite side of the Pole Star from the Dipper; a line drawn from the centre of the latter (where the handle joins the cup) through the Pole Star, about the same distance beyond it, will strike the last star of the W, which now is nearly upright (not reversed, as erroneously shown in map).

Auriga, the Charioteer, will rise later in the season in the north-eastern sky, where it will attract attention by its brightly scintillating star of first magnitude, called *Capella*, the Goat.

Capella rises in the latter part of July toward 11; middle of August to middle of September, between 10 and 8 P.M.

The Planets.

The planets, the restless wanderers, are easily distinguished from the fixed stars by their steady light, as they never, like the latter, twinkle or scintillate, except when very near the horizon.

Jupiter, " the giant planet," * will be evening star after July 9th.   He is easily recognized by his brilliant white light, with which he outshines every other planet except Venus.   He will be at his brightest on the night of October 7th, when he will be in opposition.†   A month or two before opposition (this year, July to September), he can be seen rising (east) late in the evening, while during the three months following opposition he will always be seen in the early evening somewhere between southeast and southwest. Jupiter rises after middle of July, toward 11 ; beginning of August, toward 10 ; after middle of July, toward 9 P.M.   He will be near the moon July 27th, August 23d and September 20th.

The following interesting account· we borrow from the learned and enthusiastic astronomer of the *Providence Journal :*

" It cannot be too strongly impressed upon the minds of students of the stars, that the four great planets are all approaching their perihelia (points nearest the sun), and bringing about a condition of planetary affairs that has not occurred for two thousand years.   Jupiter reaches the goal first, arriving at perihelion on the 25th of September. Such is the eccentricity of his orbit that he will then be forty-six millions of miles, or about half of the whole distance of the earth from the sun,

---

* No one can mistake this orb when it shines on a dark sky, and only Venus can be mistaken for it when seen as a morning or evening star.   Sometimes both are seen together on the twilight sky, and then Venus is generally the brighter.   Seen, however, at her brightest, her splendor scarcely exceeds that which Jupiter shines when high above the eastern horizon at midnight.—PROCTOR.

† The planets are said to be " in opposition " when the sun, earth and the planet are in a line, the earth being in the middle ; " at or in perihelion " when the planet is nearest the sun.

nearer to the great central fire than when farthest away. He is also at that time almost at his nearest point to the earth, coming into opposition with the sun eleven days after perihelion. The earth is then directly between him and the sun; but the earth is farthest from the sun in July, and will be at considerably more than her mean distance in September, when Jupiter is forty-six million miles nearer. It may easily be seen that when at opposition the earth is at or near her greatest distance, and Jupiter at his least distance, from the sun, the two planets will be almost as near together as they can be. Such will be the case next October, and the giant of the system will soon give evidence of the fact in his increasing size and brilliancy, being brighter than he has been for nearly twelve years. Jupiter, therefore, will be a source of intense interest during the coming months as he approaches and recedes from his perihelion and opposition. The great problem of the effect of his approach upon the mysterious spot-period of the sun will be first in importance. Many astronomers scout the idea of such an influence. Many more find nothing improbable in the theory that the approach of a huge mass to the sun should produce disturbance in his blazing elements, evidently in commotion from some cause, while the near correspondence in time between the maximum of the spot-period and the revolution of Jupiter favors the argument. No one doubts that the disturbed condition of the sun will be reflected on the earth in waves of intense heat, severe storms and auroral displays, or that the same influence will be felt in the same way to the system's remotest bounds."

Saturn closely follows Jupiter, and, according to our Providence authority, "holds his place not far away from his more brilliant rival. He, too, the second in size of the giant members of the brotherhood, is travelling toward his opposition with the sun, and more slowly toward perihelion, so that he is increasing in size and donning a clearer tint than the murky one that has marked his presence." He rises about half an hour later than Jupiter, toward end of July to end of August, between 11 and 9. To recognize Saturn in his glory with his moons and bright rings he must be seen through the telescope.

Venus will be the evening star after July 13th. Next to the sun and the moon, she is the most brilliant object in the heavens. She never recedes more than about 45 degrees from the sun, and is, therefore, seen by night only in the western sky in the evening, or the eastern sky in the morning, according as she is east or west of the sun. There is, therefore, seldom any difficulty in recognizing her. When at her greatest brilliancy, she can be clearly seen by the naked eye in the daytime, provided that one knows exactly where to look for her. Venus will be nearest the moon August 1st and September 5th.

Mars is travelling far off and not seen at his best, his ruddy light growing dimmer in turning down west. Mars sets during July and toward middle of August between 9.30 and 8 P.M.

TIME-TABLES

For Railroads and Steamboats running to Coney Island.

[The following tables are all that can be supplied up to date of publication. Revised tables will be given in later editions.]

RAILROADS.

Brighton Beach.—BROOKLYN, FLATBUSH, AND CONEY ISLAND RAILWAY.—Trains leave *Flatbush Avenue, Long Island Depot, Brooklyn,* hourly from 6.30 to 9.15 A.M., and from 9.15 A.M. to 9.45 P.M. half hourly. Separate trains run from *Bedford* half hourly from 11.34 A.M. to 9.34 P.M.

Trains *from Brighton Beach* for Flatbush Avenue leave at 6.40, 7.40, 8.40, 9.10, 9.40, 10.10, 10.40, 11.10 A.M. ; 12.10, 12.40, 1.10, 1.40, 2.10, 2.40, 3.10, 3.40, 4.10, 4.40, 5.10, 5.40, 6.10, 6.40, 7.10, 7.40, 8.10, 8.40, 9.10, 9.40 P.M.

Trains *from Brighton Beach* for Bedford and Prospect Park leave at 6.40, 7.40, 8.40, 9.10, 9.40, 10.10, 10.40, and 11.25 A.M. ; 12.55, 1.25, 1.55, 2.25, 2.55, 3.25, 3.55, 4.25, 4.55, 5.25, 5.55, 6.25, 6.55, 7.25, 7.55, 8.25, 8.55, 9.25, 9.40 P.M.

The 6.30, 7.15, and the 6.40 and 7.40 A.M. trains do not run on Sundays.

This table may be varied from on bad days.

Flatbush Avenue, Long Island Depot, is reached *via* Flatbush Avenue cars, from Fulton Ferry, and Atlantic Avenue cars from South, Wall, and Fulton Ferries.

Bedford Station is reached *via* Grand and Roosevelt st. Ferries, by the Franklin av. cars and rapid transit trains.

Manhattan Beach.—NEW YORK AND MANHATTAN BEACH RAILROAD, *via Bay Ridge.*—The steamer D. R. Martin will leave Pier No. 1, foot of Whitehall st. (terminus of the Elevated Railroads) connecting at Bay Ridge with trains for Manhattan Beach, as follows : 9.25, 10.25, 11.25 A.M. ; 12.25, 1.25, 2.25, 3.25, 4.25, 5.25, 6.25, and 7.25 P.M. Returning, leave Manhattan Beach at 8.20, 10.20, 11.20 A.M. ; 12.20, 1.20, 2.20, 3.20, 4.20, 5.20, 6.20, 7.20, and 8.20 P.M.

Via Greenpoint.—By steamer Sylvan Grove, from foot of 23d st., E. R., 9.45. 10.45, 11.45 A.M. ; 12.45, 1.45, 2.45, 3.45, 4.45, 5.45, 6.45 P.M. Returning, leave Manhattan Beach at 7.35, 11.05 A.M. ; 12.05, 1.05, 2.05, 3 05, 4.05, 5.05, 6.05, 7.05, 8.05 P.M.

Via Brooklyn (Greenpoint Division).—Trains for Manhattan Beach leave Greenpoint at 10 A.M., and every hour thereafter until 7 P.M.

Trains from the Beach, for Greenpoint and way stations, leave at 11.05 and five minutes past each hour until 8.05 P.M.

Trains leave Humboldt st. 6 minutes, Grand st. 10 minutes, DeKalb av. 15 minutes, Myrtle av. 18 minutes, and East New York 25 minutes after leaving Greenpoint, connecting with rapid transit from Flatbush Avenue.

The Long Island Railroad Company sell tickets at Flatbush and Bedford avs., Brooklyn, and on rapid transit trains *via* Atlantic av., for Manhattan Beach.

Excursion tickets, *via* rapid transit from Flatbush av., 45 cts. ; single tickets, 25 cts.

** Steamboats will probably commence running every day, on Saturday, June 12th, from West 22d st. to Bay Ridge, connecting with regular trains for the Beach as above, leaving West 22d st. about one hour before train leaves Bay Ridge, and stop at Leroy st. and Pier 6, N. R., each way.

West Brighton Beach.—PROSPECT PARK AND CONEY ISLAND RAILROAD.—Excursion tickets, 25 cents. Special excursion tickets for women and children on all trains to Coney Island before 3 P.M., and on all returning trains before 6 P.M., 15 cents; (children under twelve, 10 cents). On and after Tuesday, June 1st, 1880, and until further notice, trains will leave the *Brooklyn Depot* (Ninth av. and Twentieth st., Greenwood), 6.30, 7.40, 9, 10 A.M., and half hourly to 1.30 P.M., and thereafter every 15 minutes until 9 o'clock P.M.

Returning, will leave *West Brighton*, 7.05, 8.10, 9.30, 10.30 A.M., and half hourly to 2 P.M., and thereafter every 15 minutes until 9.30 P.M.

On rainy days trains will only be run half hourly from 10 A.M. to 9.30 P.M.

On Sundays the first train will leave the Brooklyn Depot at 9 A.M. and West Brighton 9.30 A.M.

The following lines of horse-cars run direct to the depot:

Park and Vanderbilt Avenue line, from Fulton and Catharine Ferries *via* Prospect Park.

Adams st. and Boerum Place cars *via* City Hall and Atlantic Avenue.

The Hamilton av. Ferry and Jay, Smith, and Ninth st. cars connect at Fifteenth st. with the horse-cars of this company, and passengers are carried free from Fifteenth st. to the depot.

West-End.—BROOKLYN, BATH, AND CONEY ISLAND RAILROAD.—Court st. and Third av. cars from Fulton Ferry. 35 minutes to depot.

From Hamilton Ferry, Fort Hamilton cars direct to depot in twenty minutes.

Fifth av. line *from South*, *Wall st.* and *Fulton Ferries*.

On and after May 9th, 1880, trains leave Greenwood depot, cor. Twenty-seventh st. and Fifth av. (near main entrance Greenwood Cemetery) daily at *6.20, *7.20, 8.10, 9, 9.50, 10.40, 11.30, 12.30, 1.30, 2.15, 3, 3.45, 4.30, 5.15, 6, 6.50, 7.40, †8.30 P.M.

Trains *from Coney Island*, 7.30, 8.20, 9.10, 10, 10.50, 11.40, 12.35, 1.35, 2.20, 3.05, 3.50, 4.35, 5.20, 6.05, 6.55, 7.45 P.M.

Fare, round trip, only 25 cents.

Trains marked * do not run on Sundays.

Trains marked thus † to Guntherville and way stations.

Sea Beach.—NEW YORK AND SEA BEACH ROUTE, *via Brooklyn*, from Sixty-fifth st. and Third av. Take cars of the Court st. and Third av. lines from Fulton Ferry, and the Hamilton av. line from Hamilton Ferry, connecting at Sixty-fifth st. and Third av., Bay Ridge.

Trains leave Third av. depot hourly from 9 A.M. till 2 P.M., and half hourly from 2 P.M. till 6.30 P.M.

Last train leaves Sea Beach for Third av. at 7 P.M.

Excursion tickets, between Brooklyn and Sea Beach, 20 cents. Single tickets, 15 cents. Children under 12 years of age, excursion tickets, 15 cents ; single tickets, 10 cents.

Via Bay Ridge.—Steamer Idlewild leaves foot W. 24th st., 9, 11 A.M., 1, 3, 5 P.M., and probably on Sundays hourly from 9 A.M. to 5 P.M., stopping at W. 10th st., Franklin st. and Pier 1, N.R. (stone pier) connecting at Bay Ridge for the beach.

Returning trains will leave the beach about 9.30, 11.30 A.M., 1.30, 3.30, 6 P.M., and on Sundays hourly from 9.30 A.M. to 4.30 and 6 P.M., connecting at Bay Ridge with boats for New York as above. Excursion tickets between New York and Sea Beach, 40 cents.

By Horse Cars.—*Via Jay and Smith sts. and Hamilton av. Ferry.*

Leave City Line Depot: 7, 8, 9, 9.40, 10.10, 10.40, 11.10, 11.40 A.M., 12.20, 12.40, 1.20, 2, 2.30, 3, 3.30, 4, 4.30, 5, 5.40, 6.20, 6.50, 7.20, 7.50, 8.30, 9, 9.40 P.M.

Leave Coney Island: 6, 7, 8, 9, 9.30, 10, 10.40, 11.10, 11.40, A.M.; 12.20, 12.50, 1.20, 1.50, 2.20, 3. 3.30, 4, 4.40, 5.10, 5.40, 6.10, 6.50, 7.30, 8, 8.40, 9.40 P.M.

Excursion tickets, 15 cents round trip, from City Line.

Passengers transferred free to and from Ninth av. and Fifteenth st. to City Line.

STEAMBOATS.

See also RAILROADS.

Iron Pier Direct.—Until further notice the steamers John Sylvester and Eliza Hancox will run as follows :

Leaving Twenty-second st., N. R., 9, 10, 12.15, 1.30, 3.30, 4.30.

Leaving Leroy st., 9.15, 10.15, 12.30, 1.45, 3.45, 4.45.

Leaving Pier 8, 9.30, 10.30, 12.45, 2, 4, 5.

Returning, leave Iron Pier, 10.30, 11.30, 2, 3, 5.30, 6.30.

Single tickets, 35 cents. Excursion tickets, 50 cents. With admission to Pier.

July, 1880.

Days.		Sun.		Moon.	HighWater.*	
Mo.	Week.	Rises.	Sets.	Rises.	Morn-ing.	After-noon.
		H. M.	H. M.	H. M.	H. M.	H. M.
1	Thursday	4 32	7 35	0 11	—	3 15
2	Friday	4 33	7 35	0 42	—	4 10
3	Saturday	4 33	7 35	1 18	—	5
4	**Sunday**	4 34	7 34	1 59	5 30	6
5	Monday	4 35	7 34	2 46	6 20	6 45
6	Tuesday	4 35	7 34	3 39	7	7 30
7	Wednesday	4 36	7 34	sets.	7 45	8
8	Thursday	4 36	7 33	8 12	8 30	8 45
9	Friday	4 37	7 33	8 41	9	9 30
10	Saturday	4 38	7 33	9 7	9 45	—
11	**Sunday**	4 38	7 32	9 32	10 30	—
12	Monday	4 39	7 32	9 57	11 10	—
13	Tuesday	4 40	7 31	10 23	noon.	—
14	Wednesday	4 41	7 31	10 52	—	12 30
15	Thursday	4 41	7 30	11 25	—	1 20
16	Friday	4 42	7 29	morn.	—	2 15
17	Saturday	4 43	7 29	0 6	—	3 20
18	**Sunday**	4 44	7 28	0 56	—	4 30
19	Monday	4 45	7 27	1 56	5	5 30
20	Tuesday	4 46	7 27	3 6	6	6 40
21	Wednesday	4 46	7 26	rises.	7	7 30
22	Thursday	4 47	7 25	7 52	8	8 30
23	Friday	4 48	7 24	8 23	9	9 20
24	Saturday	4 49	7 24	8 51	9 50	—
25	**Sunday**	4 50	7 23	9 17	10 40	—
26	Monday	4 51	7 22	9 44	11 30	—
27	Tuesday	4 52	7 21	10 12	noon.	—
28	Wednesday	4 53	7 20	10 43	—	1
29	Thursday	4 54	7 19	11 17	—	1 45
30	Friday	4 55	7 18	11 56	—	2 30
31	Saturday	4 56	7 17	morn.	—	3 30

Phases of the Moon: New, 7th; first quarter. 15th; full, 21st; third quarter, 28th.

* The calculations are based on Negus' " Nautical Almanac;" the minutes are averaged approximately. (Only the convenient hours are given.) For directions how to calculate from day to day see HIGH WATER, in the regular alphabet.

August, 1880.

| DAYS. | | SUN. | | MOON. | HIGH WATER.* | |
Mo.	Week.	Rises.	Sets.	Rises.	Morning.	Afternoon.
		H. M.	H. M.	H. M.	H. M.	H. M.
1	**Sunday**	4 56	7 16	0 41	—	4 30
2	Monday	4 57	7 15	1 32	5	5 30
3	Tuesday	4 58	7 14	2 28	6	6 20
4	Wednesday	4 59	7 12	3 27	6 45	7
5	Thursday	5 0	7 11	sets.	7 20	7 45
6	Friday	5 1	7 10	7 11	8	8 20
7	Saturday	5 2	7 9	7 37	8 40	9
8	**Sunday**	5 3	7 8	8 2	9 20	9 45
9	Monday	5 4	7 6	8 28	10	—
10	Tuesday	5 5	7 5	8 56	10 40	—
11	Wednesday	5 6	7 4	9 27	11 30	—
12	Thursday	5 7	7 2	10 5	noon.	—
13	Friday	5 8	7 1	10 50	—	1 15
14	Saturday	5 9	7 0	11 44	—	2 10
15	**Sunday**	5 10	6 58	morn.	—	3 15
16	Monday	5 11	6 57	0 48	—	4 20
17	Tuesday	5 12	6 56	1 59	—	5 30
18	Wednesday	5 13	6 54	3 14	6	6 30
19	Thursday	5 14	6 53	4 29	7	7 20
20	Friday	5 15	6 52	rises.	7 45	8 15
21	Saturday	5 16	6 50	7 17	8 40	9
22	**Sunday**	5 17	6 48	7 44	9 30	9 45
23	Monday	5 18	6 47	8 12	10 20	—
24	Tuesday	5 19	6 45	8 42	11	—
25	Wednesday	5 20	6 44	9 16	noon.	—
26	Thursday	5 21	6 42	9 54	—	12 35
27	Friday	5 22	6 41	10 37	—	1 10
28	Saturday	5 23	6 39	11 25	—	2
29	**Sunday**	5 24	6 38	morn.	—	3
30	Monday	5 25	6 36	0 19	—	4
31	Tuesday	5 26	6 34	1 13	—	5

Phases of the Moon: New, 5th; first quarter, 13th; full, 20th; third quarter, 27th.

* The calculations are based on Negus' "Nautical Almanac;" the minutes are averaged approximately. (Only the convenient hours are given.) For directions how to calculate from day to day see HIGH WATER, in the regular alphabet.

September, 1880.

	DAYS.		SUN.		MOON.	HIGH WATER.*	
Mo.	Week.	Rises.	Sets.	Rises.	Morning.	Afternoon.
		H. M.	H. M.	H. M.	H. M.	H. M.
1	Wednesday	5 27	6 33	2 18	5 20	5 45
2	Thursday	5 28	6 31	3 20	6 10	6 30
3	Friday	5 29	6 30	4 23	7	7 15
4	Saturday	5 30	6 28	sets.	7 35	8
5	**Sunday**	5 31	6 26	6 33	8 10	8 30
6	Monday	5 32	6 25	7 0	8 45	9 15
7	Tuesday	5 33	6 23	7 31	9 30	—
8	Wednesday	5 34	6 21	8 6	10 10	—
9	Thursday	5 35	6 20	8 54	11	—
10	Friday	5 36	6 18	9 40	noon.	—
11	Saturday	5 37	6 16	10 39	—	1
12	**Sunday**	5 38	6 15	11 47	—	2 10
13	Monday	5 39	6 13	morn.	—	3 20
14	Tuesday	5 40	6 11	0 58	—	4 20
15	Wednesday	5 41	6 10	2 11	—	5 20
16	Thursday	5 42	6 8	3 23	5 50	6 15
17	Friday	5 43	6 6	4 34	6 45	7 10
18	Saturday	5 44	6 4	rises.	7 30	8
19	**Sunday**	5 45	6 3	6 12	8 20	8 40
20	Monday	5 46	6 1	6 41	9	9 30
21	Tuesday	5 47	5 59	7 14	9 45	—
22	Wednesday	5 48	5 58	7 50	10 30	—
23	Thursday	5 49	5 56	8 32	11 15	—
24	Friday	5 50	5 54	9 2	noon.	—
25	Saturday	5 51	5 53	10 10	—	12 45
26	**Sunday**	5 52	5 51	11 6	—	1 30
27	Monday	5 53	5 49	morn.	—	2 20
28	Tuesday	5 54	5 48	0 5	—	3 20
29	Wednesday	5 55	5 46	1 6	—	4 20
30	Thursday	5 56	5 44	2 8	5	5 15

Phases of the Moon: New, 4th ; first quarter, 11th ; full, 18th ; third quarter, 26th.

* The calculations are based on Negus' "Nautical Almanac;" the minutes are averaged approximately. (Only the convenient hours are given.) For directions how to calculate from day to day see HIGH WATER, in the regular alphabet.

MEMORANDA.

THE

UNITED STATES

LIFE

INSURANCE COMPANY

IN THE CITY OF NEW YORK.

(Incorporated 1850.)

261, 262, 263, and 264 Broadway,

NEW YORK.

Assets, - - - - - - - $4,983,226.81
Surplus, - - - - - - 872,484.06

T. H. BROSNAN, President.

C. P. FRALEIGH,   *GEO. H. BUFORD,*
    Secretary.   *Actuary.*

LIBERAL AND IMPORTANT CONCESSIONS IN LIFE INSURANCE CONTRACTS.

---

*Examine the New Form of Policy issued by the United States
Life Insurance Company before insuring elsewhere.*

APPLETONS'

DICTIONARY OF NEW YORK

AND VICINITY.

A Guide on a New Plan.

Being an alphabetical Index to all Places, Societies,
Institutions, Amusements, and innumer-
able matters upon which informa-
tion is daily needed.

COMPILED BY

TOWNSEND PERCY.

———

With Maps of New York and Vicinity.

———

This Dictionary is an invaluable and indispensable guide to those visiting New York and vicinity. It imparts such information as will save strangers from being victimized by sharpers, as, by a careful study, they will feel perfectly at home in any part of the city.

———

PRICE, THIRTY CENTS.

———

D. APPLETON & CO., Publishers,

1, 3 AND 5 BOND STREET, NEW YORK.

What to Read.

A full survey of Current Literature, enabling any one, at an hour's reading, to make a discriminate selection of books for himself or his friends, or to converse intelligently on the literary topics of the day, is given in the LITERARY NEWS, issued monthly, subscription price only *fifty cents* per year.

The regular features of the journal are

Three Prize Questions

on choice of books and other literary subjects; (prizes each number, three at $5, $3 and $2;) the freshest news on books and authors; lists of new publications; courses of reading; quotations and critical comments from leading journals; characteristic extracts; sketches and anecdotes of contemporary authors, etc., etc.

Any one with taste for books or reading, no matter how limited his means or his time, can afford a subscription, and thus contribute to the promotion of good home reading.

Subscription, per year, 50 cents.

Specimen copy sent free to any address.

F. LEYPOLDT, PUBLISHER,

13 and 15 Park Row, New York.

[*Over.*